# THE ART OF PAINTING

## FROM PREHISTORY THROUGH THE RENAISSANCE

# *The Art of Painting*

## FROM PREHISTORY THROUGH THE RENAISSANCE

*edited by* PIERRE SEGHERS

*in collaboration with* JACQUES CHARPIER

*excerpts translated by* SALLY T. ABELES

*Hawthorn Books, Inc.* PUBLISHERS
NEW YORK AND LONDON

 *This book was manufactured in the United States of America and published simultaneously in Canada by Prentice-Hall, Inc. of Canada, 520 Ellesmere Road, Scarborough, Ontario. It was originally published in France under the title* L'Art de la Peinture *© 1957 by Pierre Seghers. Library of Congress Catalogue Card Number: 64-13282. Suggested decimal classification: 750.*

FIRST EDITION, *June, 1964*

## ACKNOWLEDGMENTS

*Permission to reprint passages from the following works is gratefully acknowledged. Every effort has been made to locate the copyright owners of the selections used in this book. If any credits have been inadvertently omitted they will be corrected in subsequent editions, provided notification is sent to the publisher.*

Lascaux, or the Birth of Art, *Georges Bataille, translated by Austryn Wainhouse, Éditions d'Art Albert Skira, Geneva, 1955. Reprinted by permission of Éditions d'Art Albert Skira.*

The Life of Appollonius of Tyana, *Philostratus, translated by F. C. Conybeare, 1912.* Natural History, *Pliny, translated by H. Rackham, 1945.* On Architecture, *Vitruvius, translated by Frank Granger, 1934. Reprinted by permission of Harvard University Press, Cambridge.*

The Notebooks of Leonardo da Vinci, *arranged, rendered into English and introduced by Edward MacCurdy, Reynal & Hitchcock, New York, 1938 and Jonathan Cape, London, 1938. Reprinted by permission of Harcourt, Brace & World, Inc. and by permission of the Executors of the Edward MacCurdy estate and Jonathan Cape Ltd.*

On Painting, *Leon Battista Alberti, translated by John R. Spencer, Yale University Press, 1956. Reprinted by permission Routledge & Kegan Paul, Ltd., London.*

The Various Arts, *Theophilus, translated by C. R. Dodwell, Thomas Nelson & Sons, Ltd., Edinburgh and London, and the Oxford University Press, New York. Reprinted by permission of Thomas Nelson & Sons, Ltd., Publishers.*

The Writings of Albrecht Dürer, *translated and edited by William Martin Conway, 1958. Reprinted by permission of Peter Owen, Ltd., London, and Philosophical Library, Inc., New York.*

H-0431

*We must always apologize for talking painting.*

PAUL VALÉRY

# FOREWORD

THE present anthology comprises as broad a selection as possible, within the chosen format, of theoretical writings on the subject of painting.

We have not included either critical or historical texts; for this reason the reader will not find specific exegeses in these pages on any particular painter, style, era, or school of painting except by way of example or reference. We have tried to choose excerpts that expose the essence of this art, its forms, its interior evolution, and to a certain degree its techniques.

Wherever possible, we have allowed the painters to speak for themselves. "A painter's ideas," says André Gide somewhere, "touch us as they take shape," a notion that contradicts the critical procedure of flatly judging a work only according to the dogmas, mental constructs, or systems it was built on. But would anybody really follow this procedure? Who would think of going to the *Abrégé de l'Art Poëtique Français* to find out whether Ronsard was or was not admirable, or to a letter from Poussin to M. de Chantelou to establish that painter's value? What an artist says about his art is one thing; the paintings he paints are another. And yet should we disdain theories?

For over half a century there has been a tendency to attribute artistic creation to a mystery definable only as genius, inspiration, or pure psychic automatism. Mystery there is, indeed, but not everything in an artist's expression is mysterious, no matter how much a genius he is. There are his ideas about his art, his beliefs, his biases, his personal myths and those of his time, his speculations, and his craft. That last word is troublesome for those who make art an offspring of religion, or of Religion par excellence. Does a clergyman, a mystic, or a martyr make a craft of his faith? Of course not—or at least he should not. But all religion engenders a theology and a ritual. An artist's theology is his ideas; his craft is his ritual. And artists too have their heresies, which often lead them far astray, with others following behind them, even to the point of formulating new dogmas and new ways of serving their god.

This is why, as often as possible, we have given the podium to the painters themselves. This does not mean we have included *all* great painters in this anthology; but the omissions are not of our choosing.

A painter is a man who has decided to express himself in plastic form. He is often only a man who paints. And he may write little, or badly, or he may not even consider writing. Or he may write without speaking of painting. Let us say in this connection that we have included a painter not for the *reason* that he has written but for the *subject* he has written about—his art. Little or none of the often voluminous correspondence of painters like Michelangelo, Rubens, Dürer, Poussin, Courbet, and Degas appears in this book because these writings, if they concern art at all, do not discuss the artists' painting but only certain aspects of their works, and often from a purely external standpoint. This explains some of the lacunae in the following pages.

But the reader will sometimes encounter names other than those he might want to find. These are minor masters, enjoying a place of honor in this book that museums have given them only occasionally. We have included them because they have had things to say on an art which they have indeed not executed well, things that others greater than they could also have said. We will not treat them with Gide's reserve and pretend to expect their works to confirm their words, though this sometimes occurs. Their intention was to formulate not a theory of genius but, more modest and yet more difficult, the theory of forms and colors that dominated the spirit of their times.

Further, the writings gathered here come not only from artists but also from art critics, philosophers, and writers.

Critics do not always speak just of contemporary events in painting; they sometimes ascend to the level of generalities. We have thought it well to include certain such writings here.

Philosophers often use painting to clothe their own reflections with examples, arguments, or images. This does not mean, of course, that they have made painting the central subject of every such essay, any more than have writers on scientific psychology, who have also devoted considerable attention to the problems of art. We have preferred not to broach those areas where only truth is under consideration, not even the study of illusions, which are properly in our bailiwick. Thus the reader will find no philosophic excerpts in the following pages that do not specifically concern pictorial aesthetics. In addition, we have included no works on optics, though this science deals with our subject in particular.[1]

Not until the eighteenth century did literature turn its attention to the plastic arts. The poets and romance writers of the Middle Ages seemed to hold aloof from them. It was the feeling of the times that words should be almost exclusively descriptive, and in view of this the poet rivaled the painter; painting his own subjects with words, the writer had no need to look elsewhere. But in fact painting said something entirely different from what writing said; painting was a sacred art, while writing was a profane and often heretical art.

During the Renaissance and the seventeenth century, painters and writers drew closer to each other, but they still remained distant. Here and there a versified *Art of Painting* or *Allegory on Painting* would crop up, but the artist would be expressing himself either as a painter or as a poet, most often without being either. In sum, if painting no longer fulfilled its ancient sacred function, or assumed it with greater liberties, it remained an art apart—as did all other arts. In a time when all the genres comprised by a single discipline were rigorously circumscribed, the gaps between the various disciplines could not help but widen. Certainly, one man could esteem Botticelli and Ronsard, Georges de la Tour and Racine at the same time, but no artist set about to influence another's work. This was an era of mutual respect for artistic prerogatives. Painters sought only their masters' counsel, as Racine did Father Dominique Bouhours'.

It is not surprising, then, that we find no noteworthy literary text on painting until Diderot. Artists in the eighteenth century began to shuck off the rules that had bound them. Painters conversed with poets and poets with painters, no longer ignoring each other but meeting face to face. A muse as yet nameless had just been born, and here we find signs of her presence.

WE have had to limit our choice to Western painting, despite our regret at not reproducing any texts on Oriental art, like *The Manual of Painting of the Garden as Large as a Mustard Seed,* which embodies the spirit and the age-old techniques of Chinese painting.

We have used no strict criteria in deciding to include one text and exclude another, for the reason that there are none that apply to anthologies. But nonetheless, we have not followed purely personal inclinations.

Because we were not able to dwell on the early cultures, given the limitations of both space and our knowledge, we have relied on specialized authors more capable than we of presenting a clear and informed idea of the artistic conceptions proper to these cultures.

With regard to Greco-Roman antiquity, we have studied Adolphe Reinach's collection in particular, and of the numerous excerpts he supplies we have incorporated those that best express the pictorial concerns of their times.

For the Middle Ages, we have included three of the excellent texts available: one by Dionysius of Phourna-Agrapha, on Byzantine painting; another by Theophilus, a twelfth-century monk, on the high Middle Ages in the West; and the third by Cennino Cennini, who passes on instructions doubtless inherited from Giotto.

Renaissance texts are a little more numerous. The excerpts chosen from the writings of Leon Battista Alberti, Leonardo da Vinci, and Francisco de Hollanda seemed necessarily to constitute the heart of the section devoted to that period. The first work centers on considerations that arise from the broadest and deepest humanism; the second gives us extremely varied and precise precepts; and the third reveals opinions that Michelangelo did not express in his correspondence or his poems.

With the seventeenth century, texts begin to be plentiful.

This was the era of academic discourse on painting. After much reading, we drew on the writings of Rubens, Félibien, and De Piles, whom the reader will find here in the company of Nicolas Poussin. These texts represent the major ideas in vogue in their time.

We have followed the same procedure for the eighteenth century, our choices here being Sir Joshua Reynolds, Denis Diderot, and Louis David, because it seems to us that this century, so poor in artistic treasures, finds in these men its only wealth.

The nineteenth century, on the contrary, offers us an embarrassment of riches. We have sidestepped the problem by including as many pages of as many meritorious artists as possible, whether the writings be their own or observations reported by others.

Finally, in the twentieth century, we find ourselves at grips with a multitude of writers, each professing opinions that are often militant and extreme and that rarely avoid polemics. As with a painting, we need time to judge a piece of writing, but we obviously cannot get that perspective; everything is too close to us. We have been forced to relinquish personal choice to the criterion of the importance the public, with its widely varying judgments, attributes to works and theories of our day. Under this system, we have tried to exclude ideas that are outmoded or that have not as yet proved themselves in the very narrow circle of members of the divers contemporary artistic coteries. And in fact, the painting of the last ten years does not yet seem to have produced a theory sufficiently explicit or courageous to justify inclusion in this book.

We have arranged the excerpts chronologically because this seemed to be the simplest and most helpful method possible, since it puts the writings in historic perspective. The reader will see that following the longer excerpts are numbers of quotations, some very brief and others a little fuller. These quotations were chosen with the object of throwing light on various details, but some of them express more general ideas. Their authors are both little known and very famous. In the case of the latter, they have not been included in the longer excerpts because they said little on our subject, not because their opinions have been disapproved. No personal value judgments have influenced these classifications—quite the contrary; we regret that we could not give more prominence to the words of some of the great painters.

Again, the majority of painters and theoreticians in this book did not know that an anthology like this would one day invite their participation. Many of them were too terse or too rambling, and others wrote nothing at all. It may astonish the reader that Impressionism, for example, which can claim such celebrated names as Monet, Pissarro, and Renoir, occupies so few pages, and even then the writings included are often the observations of others. And equally surprising may be the small space allocated to such vast texts as those of Élie Faure, Henri Focillon, and Bernard Berenson.

But precisely when a work was large we tended to hunt out quotations or excerpts within it that would sum up its author's thought in a condensed form. When the work was relatively short, we only suppressed details or secondary material; and when it was very brief, we included it in its entirety whenever possible, with the hope—not the fear—that other students will be led by their research to writings that have escaped us.

We would like to emphasize that this book is an anthology, not an exhaustive collection. But this has not prevented us from requisitioning a quantity of learned research. We have read a great number of books, some fruitlessly—they taught us a great deal, but contributed nothing to our undertaking. In sum, our task was not just to reap but also to winnow, for we are presenting only a small part of what we have gleaned.

Thus, we feel we will have made ourselves instruments for the most demanding curiosity, and that the reader will discover in this book numerous writings, hitherto unknown or only vaguely familiar, which will nourish his love of painting.

Some of the texts cited here belong to works long absent from our libraries. Some seem to have been neglected by art critics and historians, and are rarely referred to in other works. When parts of these writings struck us as having some merit or interest, we did not hesitate to bring them to the reader's attention, even if only briefly.

WHAT can a collection like this teach us? Above all, the great importance, the "metaphysical" quality, that men of all times and in all places have attributed to painting. It was useless for St. Augustine to reproach painting in the name of the evangelical theory of "concupiscence of the eyes" and for Pascal to look on it as "vanity"; their arguments carry little weight in relation to the unanimous favor painting has found throughout the centuries.

In China, the painter's art derives from the Tao: its function is to pierce appearances, the static aspect of things, and reveal their animating principle. A similar demand is made of painting in India, where the painter must show us Being in its truth, its dynamism, and its spiritual attraction. In Greco-Roman antiquity, Plato did indeed accuse the painter of lying, but without at all denying the necessity of painting; and Philostratus considered art to be "an invention of the gods," and that it should "put to the use of reason itself." The explanations in the Christian Middle Ages were no less definitive. Painting, under the patronage of St. Luke, was looked on as one of the means Adam left us to regain the Paradise he had lost, as an "inheritance from God," and all the authors of our excerpts exhort those who have this gift not to hoard it jealously. This mystical explanation of the function of painting gave way to a scientific explanation in the Renaissance. With Da Vinci, the whole universe, no longer just man alone, became the object of painting; and the painter was considered in essence an experimentalist with the world who sees through appearance and custom to the truth in nature. Poussin's work goes beyond this supreme naturalism into a sort of heroic psychology: man is known and mastered not only in his form but in his soul and in the ideal content of his action. In the eighteenth century, the notion of painting became more essentially "artistic," but the art nonetheless continued to strive for that highest objective: the expression of human passions in their transcendental aspect and insofar as they determine genius. This tendency grew stronger in the nineteenth century, and Delacroix did not hesitate to call what he saw in the painter's art a "magic" that carries the viewer of a masterpiece beyond the form and the visible into a state of indescribable ecstasy.

From Delacroix on, if schools of painting mushroomed and denounced each other all around, it was for the specific purpose of granting painting strict autonomy, of establishing for painting a goal within itself. It was no longer a question of assigning the art one or another place in the hierarchy of human activity; painting became necessary and sufficient unto itself, unlike any other activity—a fundamental spiritual need that nothing can stop one from satisfying. Painters know this well, those who live painting like Christ's passion. In their own ways. Van Gogh and Gauguin were crucified men. And Manet himself, the wise Manet, the ironic artisan, who declared that the most beautiful subject for his painting would be Christ crucified, might well have had the notion in the back of his atheistic head that the pain of his model translated the battle he fought as a painter for the essential Idea of painting.

Thus, in the modern world, painting became a sort of redemption of the visual mediocrities of existence, to the point where the state opened its temples, the museums, to the most heretical, the most demoniacal of painters. Painting today is nowhere excluded. A whole hierarchy of teachers and curators officiate in its name. There is still academism, but it does not block the temple gates. The ordinary citizen, yesterday covered with insults that he knew how to repay in vengeance, today buys and brags about what his father cursed. A painting that began its life obscurely but a few hours ago quickly emerges from the catacombs to take its seat in the public square. This may not happen without a certain risk—that the world is using this ultimate ruse of bestowing its greatest favors on the artist the better to chain him to itself —but this is not the place to discuss the point.

ONCE these pages are read, what should we think of the writers' more-or-less stated ambition to define the essence of painting? Have they achieved their aim; and must we reject what we believed to be works of genius if they do not correspond at all to the particular definition of painting that we have come to accept? Will we discover that this art has not yet found a thinker who, clearing away the hostilities of different schools and periods, can show us the necessary and sufficient condition of painting? Or must we despair of discerning among all these works, antagonistic to each other, a common denominator other than the pleasure we receive when we look at them?

Some of these writers have formulated answers as crude as the dictionary definition of poetry—"Poetry: the art of versifying." So Isidorus tells us, across two thousand years, that a picture is "the representation of an object," and Maurice Denis calls it "essentially a plane surface covered with colors arranged in a certain order." To have painting, then, is it enough to reproduce an apple or arrange a few blobs of color according to one of those slightly disciplined chance occurrences that happen even in nature?

And yet, one idea has obsessed painters of different ages, and deserves not to be neglected—that painting is the imitation in forms and colors of the *real.* This idea was universally accepted until the advent of abstract art, and even then only the conception of reality, not the desire to imitate it, changed. The idea obsessed Da Vinci as it did Cézanne, Poussin as Chardin, the Impressionists as the Surrealists (who aspire to "the *real* functioning of thought"). The real is sometimes God and sometimes man, sometimes sights in nature and sometimes the very structure of things. Neither sacred painting nor profane escapes it, both disregarding appearances in order to attain a reality hidden from our senses that the spirit alone can reveal.

And perhaps in reflecting on that obsession with truth (instead of on truth itself, which is so variable) we will be able to discover the justification for the act of painting.

If the painter wants the truth, it is because it is not given to him. The most realistic painting cannot gainsay that fact. Even were a painter satisfied with common reality, he must, in spite of himself, re-present it, give it a second expression. And these disciples of reality resort to a lie: "*Pictura autem dicta quasi fictura,*" says Isidorus—to paint is to feign. And that fiction which results is obtained by means of forms and colors.

Some, though, attempt to make ends of their means. They adjudge reality (of whatever variety) unsuitable for painting, and thus strip their work of all lies—but also of all effectiveness. Notions of harmony, musicality, rhythm, and the like are inadequate to define the act of painting.

Man is indissolubly linked with the world and his own individuality. He cannot ignore his condition. He can transcend it, but it is always there, along with the forms and figures that populate it; this is why St. John Chrysostom insisted that an artist use human traits to represent the inaccessible divinity. As a result, the most abstract concept takes on flesh in a painting. Painting is the incarnation of a reality beyond the range of our senses, or the reincarnation of what is within their ken.

A painter who tries to achieve pure visuality sets his viewer (and himself) before an untenable contradiction. He demands the impossible—that they forget they are both men. Hence that particular frustration one feels before paintings that "don't mean anything," for we are irresistibly tempted to give them a meaning, to establish a rapport between them and ourselves and them and the world; and this they are not susceptible of by nature.

That such art could be conceived and developed, despite this contradiction, comes perhaps from a false concept of aesthetic "logic," according to which the artist must of necessity carry out to their ultimate consequences the trends that predate him. Because in painting these trends are expressed as a systematic withdrawal from objects, the painter infers that objects should disappear completely from painting. The inference comes not from a deep concern—that aesthetic concern that presages or co-occurs with every great artistic creation—but from superficial reasoning based purely on contingencies of art history.

It is noteworthy that at the same time the abstract or nonrepresentational artist often displays a bad conscience, as it were, a kind of nostalgia for the real. He seems to search for justifications in the material or mental world. He points out natural forms which, though they have not inspired his work, bear some chance resemblance to it; he gives his pictures image titles, subjects which he has discovered after the fact and which he feels the need to define in verbal terms since they have no plastic definition.

For this notion of the real, however vague and variable

it may be, is tenacious. And all painting intends to be the knowledge of what is; as visual art, it shares the preponderance that sight exercises over all our other powers of perception. St. Augustine, who disapproved of painting, gave it this fine homage:

> To see is . . . the task proper to the eyes. But we use this word even with regard to the other senses when we apply them to the act of knowing. We do not say "Listen how that sparkles," or "Feel how that shines," or "Taste how that glitters," or "Touch how that dazzles." It is the word *see* that fits all these expressions. And again, we say not only "See what a light!" (which the eyes alone can do), but also "See what a sound, see what an odor, see what a taste, see how hard!"[2]

Thus painting, which has also been called a silent language, has a universal function that it derives from the ascendency of sight over all our other senses: to manifest as categorically as possible *what is*—in us and outside us, visible and invisible.

Yet we should not take this as a conclusive apology for realism. Plato says that painting is *eikastikē,* but also *phantastikē,* which means approximately the art of copying and the art of imagining. *Eikastikē* alone is inadequate because it would exclude the real from what it would represent, would allow no place for the man who has seen reality and wants to show it to other men. Besides, realism in painting is *ipso facto* impossible. Fernand Léger suggested that if ten realistic painters painted the same object in the same light, from the same angle, and so forth, they would produce as many different images of the object. This is not to say that their ability to strike a likeness would be greater or less, but that whatever a man puts his hand to shows that man's mark, and this mark necessarily differs from what we say is similar.

Certainly, the history of painting is subject to cycles, and periodically *eikastikē* or *phantastikē* will influence painters' work more strongly. But in all valid painting, never is either entirely absent from the act of artistic creation. Painting must always be faithful, in whatever way it chooses, to this double principle, if it is not to be mutilated by the exclusion of a part of that whole truth composed of the perceived and the perceiver. Today's philosophers have completed Berkeley's adage, *esse est percipi,* with the addition, *vel percipere*—to be is to be perceived or to perceive. The task of the painter, as of every artist, is to suppress the alternative by commingling these two terms in the aesthetic act. Then being is revealed in its fullness: it is thing and it is man.

In sum, only in facing reality and imposing his own vision on it does the painter create a valid work which is not a pure negation of himself or of the world and which is humanly justified. Of course, this essential condition of painting is in no wise sufficient, but without it the essence of painting, or at least the essence of pictorial genius, would escape us. For the lesson to be drawn from the following pages is other than whether a man is a great painter or not. We will doubtless never know what makes a painter great. But we can glimpse what makes him *not* great, and this is already a good deal.

# *Contents*

## *The Renaissance*

# *List of Illustrations*



***All illustrations are reproduced through the courtesy of Istituto Italiano d'Arti Grafiche, Bergamo, Italy***

# INTRODUCTION

IT goes without saying that we have no material, written or pictorial, to give us information on the rock paintings of the paleolithic period, like those at Lascaux, Eyzies-de-Tayac, Altamira, and elsewhere.[1] The graphic quality of these drawings, whose discovery caused as much excitement among the public at large as among scholars, testifies to an extremely well-developed artistic sense. The murals inspire fascinated speculation, nourished and developed by the mystery that still surrounds the men of that time (some 40,000 years ago). For this reason, it would have been difficult to pass over these ancestors of documented art history, and so we have included some excerpts from Georges Bataille's *Lascaux, ou la Naissance de l'Art*. Georges Bataille is not a student of prehistory; he is a writer and philosopher, and he is also a profound art lover. Thoroughly acquainted with the arts despite his young years, and particularly devoted to prehistoric rock painting, Bataille puts forth here only the most legitimate hypotheses. He thinks that art is always a transgression by the artist on society's taboos and an aspiration to produce the prodigious, that is, to create a phenomenon: the work of art, which exemplifies human liberty in the measure that the work is play and no longer work, can have a logical, a pragmatic end, but it can also incorporate a value that overflows these categories. Thus, without casting doubt on the magical "reasons" generally attributed to prehistoric painting, Georges Bataille sees in it also—and above all—the beginning of *art,* properly speaking, in the purest, most disinterested, freest sense of the word. And indeed, the elegant horses, the stylized oxen, the charging mammoths, the agile deer bounding around the walls of the caverns seem to predicate of those who placed them there as well as of ourselves an aesthetic pleasure that the magical usage which is quite properly attributed to them does not encompass.

From Greek and Roman antiquity we have not inherited treatises on painting comparable to the heritage poetry has received, for example, in the works of Aristotle and Horace. The problems of painting did occupy the minds of the classic thinkers to some extent, but it took some digging to find the scattered reflections they expressed on this art in works spanning many centuries. This was the chief concern of Adolphe Reinach, nephew of Salomon Reinach, who collected, translated, and commented on these *Textes Grecs et Latins relatifs à l'Histoire de la Peinture Ancienne.* We have chosen excerpts from this rich and valuable collection that will give the reader some general (and sometimes rather detailed) notions on the aesthetics and techniques of antiquity. We will see that these writers classified all of painting under the idea of imitation, but they also knew quite well that all art uses artifice to persuade us of "reality." This is what Plato called *phantastikē.* Aristotle did not hesitate to admit that the painter is correct in embellishing the real. Cicero praised the painter's ability to see a richness in things that escape the rest of us. Horace sided with audacity. Quintilian scorned copiers of nature. Philostratus granted the painter the right of imagination. And St. John Chrysostom insisted that the tendency to overburden a work is a dangerous scruple that limits the painter's work. It would doubtless be absurd to read into these considerations a forecast of modern painting; but they do contain a more or less apparent condemnation of the pure and simple desire to respect nature.

Philostratus found it unseemly to think that the god Apollo could descend from his chariot "to amuse himself painting trifles." Nor would the artists of the Middle Ages have entertained the notion that their God would do such a thing. Nonetheless, for them, all painting was religious, inseparable from divinity. Painting was a sacred art par excellence, imbued with mystical values and forms, anecdotal in that it referred to events recorded in Scripture, but detached from any naturalistic concept. For the Christian artist, there was nothing in nature that merited representation for itself. Nature intervened in his work only as a manifestation of divine power. It was itself a creation of the Supreme Artist's which it would have been a sin to try to rival. Thus, we do not find in the following writings a theory of painting in the sense of a collection of reflections on how to conquer reality or on the aesthetic foundation of that art. Nor do we find the personality of the artist expressing itself. For the medieval painter, such problems were already resolved by theology, and he was totally in the service of his religion. His art (at least, when he spoke of it) is thus not endowed with the appearance of an intrinsic meditation. He limited himself—and this was everything to him—to enunciating a great number of prescriptions whose purpose was to give his work a maximum of concrete qualities: solidity, splendor, perpetuity, and the like. But we must point out that Dionysius, monk of Phourna-Agrapha, Theophilus, and Cennini all three considered painting as a path to mystical knowledge inherited from the Golden Age, and as a *gift,* not a collection of received formulas. Thus, despite the strict codification of its themes and techniques, painting in the Middle Ages was no less a matter of personal talent. This is obvious, of course, and no one has ever thought that an artist could be just an artisan; but it is good to recall this fact in a time when a certain ideology tends to condemn the very principle of artistic individuality, without having at its service, moreover, the universality and depth of the Christian myth.

If Renaissance painters continued to paint religious subjects, they did so in a different spirit from that of the preceding centuries. They discovered nature and man; they devoted themselves primarily to observing what was before their eyes, which explains their great concern with perspective, with the play of light and shadow, with colors, anatomy, and even the psychology of their models. Before these interests were formulated into techniques, they grew out of a naturalistic, humanist, and even scientic spirit. As a result, the Renaissance was a period of great pictorial instruction. The treatises of the Middle Ages were artisans' manuals; those of the fifteenth and sixteenth centuries were veritable summas of painting. The art of painting was elevated above all other arts, and the painter became a sort of universal man, superior to the poet and the peer of the thinker. Leonardo was the perfect incarnation of this superiority and universality. But he was not just a theoretician of painting; he took up all the details of his art, and spoke as a craftsman. His teaching, encompassing the largest ideas and the humblest precepts, is not limited to his own time. Every later school, including the most modern, can profit by it.

# THE ART OF PAINTING

## FROM PREHISTORY THROUGH THE RENAISSANCE

# *Prehistoric Times*

HAD NOT THE LIFE THEY LED AMPLY
LIFTED THESE MEN TO HEIGHTS
OF EXUBERANCE, OF JOY, THEY COULD NOT HAVE
REPRESENTED IT WITH SUCH PERSUASIVE FORCE.

*Bataille*

# PREHISTORIC PAINTING

## *Lascaux or the Birth of Art*

*The birth of art*

FOR when speaking of periods more remote than the Upper Paleolithic Age, we cannot strictly refer to *man*. The caves were occupied by a being who resembled a man in one sense: he worked, had what students of prehistory call an industry: there were places set aside for the hewing of stone. But never was there any making of a "work of art". He would not have known how to go about such a thing and furthermore, it would appear, he had no desire to try. . . . It is the man who dwelt in this cave of whom for the first time and with certainty we may finally say: he produced works of art; he is of our sort. It is easy to add that the resemblance is imperfect: many elements are lacking in him, and we notice their absence. But perchance these elements really do not have all the importance we assign them. We ought rather to stress the fact he possessed a decisive virtue: a creative virtue which, today, has ceased to be necessary.

"LASCAUX MAN" *created, and created out of nothing, this world of art in which communication between individual minds begins.*

FOLLOWING along the rock walls, we see a kind of cavalcade of animals . . . But this animality is nonetheless *for us* the first sign, the blind unthinking sign and yet the living intimate sign, of *our* presence in the real world.

IT must be admitted: our first reaction to Lascaux is obscure, half mute, only half intelligible. It is the most ancient, the first of responses; the night of time through which it comes is pierced by no more than uncertain glimmers of faint light. We know next to nothing of the men who left behind only these elusive shadows, framed within almost nothing, unprovided with any explanatory background. We know only that these shadows are beautiful to look at, to our eyes quite as beautiful as our galleries' finest paintings. But about these we do at least know something: dates, names of the painters, the subject, the intention behind the work. We are familiar with the customs and ways of life they are related to, we may read chronicles of the times in which they were produced. They are not at all, as are these at Lascaux, the issue of a world about which our information is confined to the knowledge that there were few resources in those days, that man was limited to hunting wild beasts and picking wild berries; for stone or bone tools and graves tell us but little of the elementary civilization he had developed. Even the date of the Lascaux paintings cannot be reckoned unless one is willing to be content with estimates allowing a leeway, this way or that, of a good ten thousand years. We can recognize almost every animal depicted; magic, we usually suppose, motivated the painters' efforts. But we have no way of knowing the exact place these figures held in the beliefs and the rites of those persons who lived many thousand years before recorded history began. We are unable to do more than relate and compare them to other paintings—or various kinds of art-objects—belonging to the same periods and the same regions, and these other works of art turn out to be just as mysterious. These figures do exist in some great quantity: the Lascaux Cave alone contains hundreds of them, and there are many more in other grottoes in France and Spain. Taken as a whole, Lascaux' paintings, while perhaps not the oldest, form the finest and most intact group we have. Indeed, we may say that nothing tells us more about the life and thought of those men who were the first to have the power to deliver themselves of that profound but enigmatic utterance, a detached work of art. These paintings before us are miraculous, they communicate a strong and intimate emotion. Yet for all that they are only the more unintelligible. We have been advised to relate them to the incantations of hunters who thirsted to kill the game they subsisted upon, but it is these figures, and not the hunger of the hunters, which stir us. And so we are left painfully in suspense by this incomparable beauty and the sympathy it awakes in us.

*The men of Lascaux were rich*

STANDING before Lascaux' frescoes, rich beyond measure with the energy of animal life, how can we attribute to the men who conceived them a poverty this energy refutes? Had not the life they led amply lifted these men to heights of exuberance, of joy, they could not have represented it with such persuasive force. But, above all, we see that life's impact moved them in humane directions: this vision of animality is humane. Why? Because the life it incarnates is transfigured in the painting, made fair, made beautiful and for this reason made sovereign, exalted far above all imaginable poverty.

*The part genius played*

ODD, the way some strove to compare the Cave's masterworks to children's scribblings . . . But our youngsters benefit from supervision and guidance; the men of the Old Stone Age were on their own. Abandoned upon earth, they make one think of those young humans who are now and then brought up by wolves: but they whom a rare misfortune entrusts to the solicitude of wild animals are little apt to surmount the backwardness sure to result from their privations. Earliest men are distinguished by an extraordinary achievement: unaided, alone—through the effort of generations, to be sure—, they elaborated a human world.

*Where prohibitions are overstepped in play, in art, in religion*

IN Lascaux Man's mind, magic must have had a rôle similar to the one it occupies in the minds of the peoples studied by ethnology and ancient history. It would however be well to protest against the habit of overweighting this will to take, or invoke, efficacious action. We must finally admit that, in every ritual operation, the seeking after a specific end is never but one amongst a number of its operators' motives: these motives derive from the whole of reality, its religious and sensible (aesthetic) sides alike. In every case, they imply what has always been art's purpose: to create a sensible reality whereby the ordinary world is modified in response to the desire for the extraordinary, for the marvelous, a desire implicit in the human being's very essence. Any given work of art's specific intention is thus of small account if one considers the constancy and universality of that overriding purpose. Is it a true work of art where it is absent?

WHY, groping in these obscure places, must we plant expectations everywhere? why, when, precisely, it is plain that the art of imitating the outer aspect of animals by means of painting or engraving *could not have been put to use before it came into being* and, in order *to be,* had first *to be found* in the course of accident, chance, or play.

*Prohibition and transgression*

A work of art, a sacrifice contain something of an irrepressible festive exuberance that overflows the world of work, and clash with, if not the letter, the spirit of the prohibitions indispensable to safeguarding this world. Every work of art, in isolation, possesses a meaning independent of the desire for the prodigal, a desire each has in common with all the rest. But we may say in advance that a work of art in which this desire cannot be sensed, in which it is faint or barely present, is a mediocre work. Similarly, there is a specific motive behind every sacrifice: an abundant harvest, expiation, or any other logical objective; nonetheless, in one way or another, every sacrifice has its cause in the quest for a sacred instant that, for an instant, puts to rout the profane time in which prohibitions guarantee the possibility of life.

*Description of the cave: the main hall*

WE know nothing whatever of those gatherings in a Hall which contains space for, let us say, a hundred persons, even a few more if crowded together. But we may suppose that the painted caverns, which were not used for dwelling places (only those parts near freely circulating air sometimes housed permanent occupants), exerted a powerful attraction. All men share an instinctive dread and awe of complete darkness. That terror is "sacred", obscure light suggests what is religious: the Cavern's aspect intensified the impression of magical power, of penetration into an inaccessible domain which, at that time, painting strove to create. The caves still have about them something that seizes, spellbinds the visitor, quickens his pulse: these places are still able to cause an inner distress not at all unlike the anguish connected with sacred rites. . . .

To be successful, the dread-inspiring spell the painter sought to cast did not, however, require large audiences. Figures were often painted (or graved) in galleries too narrow to admit a sizable assembly; and sometimes—as for example in the "Room of the Felines" at Lascaux—the artist worked in recesses and nooks so cramped that one man has trouble edging his way inside . . . But large numbers probably met in Lascaux' Main Hall, so capable by itself of arousing feelings of religious dread. At any rate, we must remark the painters' apparently constant concern to leave intact an already simple and redoubtable majesty, forcefully expressed by the huge bulls overmastering the sanctuary.

IF some element other than hunger, if play, if dream slipped its way into the painting of the Cave, should we not decidedly guard against an idea which would turn Lascaux into a triumph of logic, which would make short shrift of that free impulse, that airy gesture, essentially motivated by nothing, suggested by fantasy, which, when missing from art, leaves art bereft of charm?

*Man clad in the glory of the beast*

WHAT brings us to an amazed, bewildered halt and holds us there is this extreme self-effacement of man before the animal—and of man just turning into a human. The fact the represented animal was man's prey and food does nothing to lessen this humility. Reindeer Age Man left us an at once wondrous and faithful picture of the animal, but wherever he pictures himself he almost always conceals his features behind an animal mask. He achieved positive virtuosity as a draughtsman, but disdained to portray his own face; if he confessed to having the human form, he hid it the same instant—as though he were ashamed of his face. As though when wishing to designate himself he had instantly to put on the mask of another.

*Lascaux's place in the history of art*

THIS point is crucial: Reindeer Age art was informed not by tradition, but by nature: its rule was faithfully to imitate nature. Just *what* rules it received may be of no great importance. But this is: the norm came from *outside*. Which means that, in itself, the work of art was free, not hinged to, not yoked by the methods and manners which might have determined its form from *within*—and which would have trimmed it to fit convention. . . . The Reindeer Age which by and large saw few changes in ways of living, seems primarily to have responded (but not in compliance with convention) to the fundamental and exterior idea of nature. Ways of doing and making things existed and, without any doubt, the men of those times handed them down from one generation to the next, but they did not dictate the work of art's form or breathe life into it. That routine weighed so lightly need not surprise us if we remember that these were earliest steps: no rut had yet formed to imprison the adventurer. In its beginnings, art had unavoidably to summon forth that leap of free spontaneity which we usually call genius. At Lascaux it is this free movement we sense most deeply, and that is why, writing about cave-art, I have spoken of art's beginnings. We can do no better than roughly date these paintings. But whatever their real date, they were something new: out of nothing, they created the world they figure.

AT Lascaux, gazing at these pictures, we sense that *something is stirring, something is moving.* That something touches us, we are stirred by it, as though in sympathy with the rhythms of a dance; from this passionate movement emanates the beauty of the paintings. They are, we recognize, the individual's free communication with the world around him, they are man's reaching out to touch his kind, whose inner wealth he is just discovering. This intoxicating emotion of dance was always strong enough to lift art above the subordinated tasks which man accepted to perform at the behest of religion or magic. Conversely, the harmony of the individual with the world around him invites him to undertake the transfigurations of art—and they are the transfigurations of genius.

*Note on the techniques of prehistoric painting*

THE art of painting in those earliest ages attained a refinement and a richness of means that is both extraordinary and disconcerting. To be sure there was not much choosing amongst surfaces to paint upon: the painters simply used the smoothest areas of the rock walls. It is not likely that Upper Paleolithic Franco-Cantabrian artists did out-of-doors rupestral painting. On the other hand, they could have, and all they did could have vanished; we incline, however, to think the contrary, for more or less numerous examples of out-of-doors painting have survived from the Spanish Levant whose art was roughly contemporary with the northerly region's.

Pigments were employed just as they came from their natural sources, ground fine and thinned with water or mixed with fatty substances. Paint was either liquid or paste-like. Most colors were based on mineral oxides: blacks and browns were furnished by manganese, red ochre by iron oxide. These substances, furthermore, had been utilized as far back as the Middle Paleolithic by Neanderthal Man, and we imagine he employed them for painting his body. But only in the Upper Paleolithic did man begin to use these materials in the representation of natural forms. At the very beginning, fingers applied the paint. Later on, a variety of means was used: pads or wads of vegetable matter, tufts of hair, the chewn or shredded ends of sticks. Besides these, Reindeer Age Man, particularly at Lascaux, very certainly employed a process still in use amongst the Australian aborigines of today: it consists in putting colored powder into a hollow tube and in blowing it over a moistened surface. It was thus early painters produced the stencilled hands which are fairly frequently met with in most of the caves: one hand was pressed flat against the wall, and the color was blown on around it. At Lascaux this process was commonly used for applying flat shades to a surface—one thinks especially of the horses' manes which look vaporous, whose edges are not sharp. We do not know how they managed in this way to compose whole masterfully executed groups. They may have used hollow bones or reeds. Such bones, filled with pigment, have been found in the course of excavations.

The outline was sometimes sketched with the aid of a very fine dark line. But this contour delimiting a flat painted area may just as well have been put in afterwards. At any rate, when at Lascaux a form was circumscribed by an engraved outline, that outline came last. Figures were sometimes gone over again long after they had been done for the first time: form and color might then be modified. (Georges Bataille)

# *Greco-Roman Antiquity*

PAINTING IS AN IMAGE THAT PRESENTS THE APPEARANCE OF AN OBJECT—TO PAINT IS TO FEIGN. ALL IMAGES ARE FICTION, NOT REALITY. . . .

*Isidorus*

# PLINY THE ELDER

## *Natural History*

THE question as to the origin of the art of painting is uncertain. . . . The Egyptians declare that it was invented among themselves six thousand years ago before it passed over into Greece—which is clearly an idle assertion. As to the Greeks, some of them say it was discovered at Sicyon, others in Corinth, but all agree that it began with tracing an outline round a man's shadow and consequently that pictures were originally done this way, but the second stage when a more elaborate method had been invented was done in a single colour and called monochrome, a method still in use at the present day. (XXXV, 5)

*The aesthetics of ancient painting*

EVENTUALLY art differentiated itself, and discovered light and shade, contrast of colours heightening their effect reciprocally. Then came the final adjunct of shine, quite a different thing from light. The opposition between shine and light on the one hand and shade on the other was called contrast, while the juxtaposition of colours and their passage one into another was termed attunement. (XXXV, 11)

TO paint bulk and the surface within the outlines, though no doubt a great achievement, is one in which many have won distinction, but to give the contour of the figures, and make a satisfactory boundary where the painting within finishes, is rarely attained in successful artistry. For the contour ought to round itself off and so terminate as to suggest the presence of other parts behind it also, and disclose even what it hides. (XXXV, 36)

IT is a curious and truly remarkable fact that we appreciate an artist's last works and the pictures he has left unfinished more than we do his finished works. . . . In them we see the traces of the design and catch the artist's very thought.

(APELLES) said that in all respects his achievements and those of Protogenes were on a level, or those of Protogenes were superior, but that in one respect he stood higher, that he knew when to take his hand away from a picture—a noteworthy warning of the frequently evil effects of excessive diligence. (XXXV, 36)

## ISIDORUS OF PELUSIUM

PAINTING is an image that presents the appearance of an object—to paint is to feign. All images are fiction, not reality . . . . (*Orig.*, XIX, 16)

## ARISTOTLE

IF one paints confusedly, even if in the most beautiful colors, it will not give so much pleasure as a picture painted simply in white. (*Poet.*, VI, 15)

WE must imitate good portrait painters, who, when they want to reproduce their own features even though they are thinking only of making an exact resemblance, paint themselves all the better. (*Poet.*, XV, 10)

THE best copyist will draw praise only if he aims at imitating what is most beautiful. (*Magn. Mor.*, I, 1, 19[20])

[THE CREATOR] begins by drawing all the outlines; then he chooses colors and shadows and highlights as if god were really a painter of nature. In this same way do painters, after they have made the draft of their drawing, give their colors to the being they want to represent. (*De Anim. gen.*, II, 6)

HERE is a way to give colors their value: it consists of making them glow in relation to each other, as painters do sometimes, by putting another color on one that is brighter. (*De Sensu,* 3)

## PLATO

*The Stranger:* In the art of imitating, I first distinguish the art of copying. Now, copying is reproducing the proportions of a model in length, breadth, and depth; it is further the addition to each part of the drawing of the colors appropriate to each so as to achieve a perfect imitation.

*Theaetetus:* Indeed! Don't all those who imitate try to do the same thing?

*The Stranger:* No, at least not those who paint or sculpt on a large scale. You know, of course, that if they gave true-to-life proportions to the beautiful figures they design, the upper parts would look too small to us and the lower too large, because we see the former from a distance and the latter from close up. Our artists of today, therefore, without worrying about the truth, measure the proportions of their figures not according to reality but according to appearances.

*Theaetetus:* That is in fact how they proceed. Now, isn't it correct to call this first kind of imitation a copy?

—Yes.

—And as we've already said, mustn't we call that part of the art of imitating the art of copying?

—We must call it that.

*The Stranger:* But listen. What shall we call that which seems to resemble the beautiful, because the perspective has been handled with an eye to the beautiful, but which, when you have the time to contemplate it at leisure, no longer resembles the object whose image it is? Because it seems to have a real resemblance, isn't it a phantom?

—So it is.

—Isn't this, then, a considerable part of painting, and, in general, of the art of imitating?

—Undeniably. And wouldn't it be exactly accurate to call phantasmagoria the art that produces a phantom instead of a faithful copy?

—So it would be.

—Then, these are the two kinds of the art of making semblances I was speaking about: the art of copying and phantasmagoria.

IT is as if someone found us painting human figures and reproached us for not putting the brightest colors on the loveliest places in the figure—for not coloring the eyes, though they are the most beautiful part, red instead of black. It seems we could justify ourselves fairly well by saying, "But my friend, we cannot make the eyes so beautiful that they no longer seem to be eyes, and the same with the other parts; look and see if we haven't produced a beautiful whole by giving each part the color that suits it." (*Sophist.*, 23, p. 235e–236b)

## DIONYSIUS OF HALICARNASSUS

WE have old paintings whose colors are worked with utter simplicity and which have no variety in their tones, but the lines are drawn to perfection, giving these works great charm. This purity of line was lost little by little, and was replaced by a more sophisticated technique, a skillful differentiation of light and shadow, and all the resources of that rich use of color to which these paintings owe their effect. (*De Isaeo jud.*, 4)

## CICERO

HOW many fine details that our eye cannot grasp do painters see in shadows and models! (*Acad.*, II, 7)

In paintings, some like savage, chaotic, dark works plunged in shadows; others like works that are bright, gay, embellished with the most beautiful colors. (*Oratims.*, 11)

## QUINTILIAN

A painting in which nothing is given value cannot excel. This is why painters, even when they put many figures into a single picture, separate them with sufficient space so that the shadow of one will not fall on the body of another. (VIII, 5, 26)

ALTHOUGH some painters limit their efforts to dividing their paintings with lines and according to dimensions, it is shameful only to copy what one wants to imitate. (X, 2, 6)

ALTHOUGH painting is mute and its appearance is always the same, it can penetrate the most intimate feelings so well that it sometimes seems to surpass the power of the word. (XI, 3, 67)

## HORACE

PAINTERS and poets alike always have the right to try anything. We know this, and claim it [for ourselves, poets], and grant it [to painters] by turns. (*Ars Poet.*, 9–11)

## PLUTARCH

ONE must thus put radiant, glowing events in the forefront of his thoughts, as one does with colors in a painting, and hide, push into the background everything somber, since it is not possible to wipe it out and discard it entirely.

(*De tranquil. an.*, 15)

IT is in the nature of light to make objects come forth and stand clear, while a dark color seems to produce an effect of shadow and depth . . . .

EVERYTHING with a dark cast has a concave appearance; this is why painters paint an object in light colors when they want to give it relief; when they want to achieve an effect of hollowness and depth, they paint it in dark colors.

(*Quaest. de Arati signis*, 2)

## PHILOSTRATUS

### *Life of Apollonius of Tyana*

APOLLONIUS said: "O Damis, is there such a thing as painting?" "Why, yes," he answered, "if there be any such thing as truth." "And what does this art do?" "It mixes together," replied Damis, "all the colours there are, blue with green, and white with black, and red with yellow." "And for what reason," said the other, "does it mix these? For it isn't merely to get a colour, like dyed wax." "It is," said Damis, "for the sake of imitation, and to get a likeness of a dog, or a horse, or a man, or a ship, or of anything else under the sun;

and what is more, you see the sun himself represented, sometimes borne upon a four horse car, as he is said to be seen here, and sometimes again, traversing the heaven with his torch, in case you are depicting the ether and the home of the gods." "Then, O Damis, painting is imitation?" "And what else could it be?" said he: "for if it did not effect that, it would be voted to be an idle playing with colours." "And," said the other, "the things which are seen in heaven, whenever the clouds are torn away from one another, I mean the centaurs and stag-antelopes, yes, and the wolves too, and the horses, what have you got to say about them? Are we not to regard them as works of imitation?" "It would seem so," he replied. "Then, Damis, God is a painter, and has left his winged chariot, upon which he travels, as he disposes of affairs human and divine, and he sits down on these occasions to amuse himself by drawing these pictures, as children make figures in the sand." Damis blushed, for he felt that his argument was reduced to such an absurdity. But Apollonius, on his side, had no wish to humiliate him, for he was not unfeeling in his refutations of people, and said: "But I am sure, Damis, you did not mean that; rather that these figures flit through the heaven not only without meaning, but, so far as providence is concerned, by mere chance; while we who by nature are prone to imitation rearrange and create them in these regular figures." "We may," he said, "rather consider this to be the case, O Apollonius, for it is more probable, and a much sounder idea." "Then, O Damis, the mimetic art is twofold, and we may regard the one kind as an employment of the hands and mind in producing imitations, and declare that this is painting, whereas the other kind consists in making likenesses with the mind alone." "Not twofold," replied Damis, "for we ought to regard the former as the more perfect and more complete kind being anyhow painting, and a faculty of making likenesses with the help both of mind and hand; but we must regard the other kind as a department of that, since its possessor perceives and imitates with the mind, without having the delineative faculty, and would never use his hand in depicting its objects." "Then," said Apollonius, "you mean, Damis, that the hand is disabled by a blow or by disease?" "No," he answered, "but it is disabled, because it has never handled pencil nor any instrument of colour, and has never learned to draw.'' ''Then,'' said the other, ''we are both of us, Damis, agreed that man owes his mimetic faculty to nature, but his power of painting to art. And the same would appear true of plastic art. But, methinks, you would not confine painting itself to the mere use of colours, for a single colour was often found sufficient for this purpose by our older painters; and as the art advanced, it employed four, and later, yet more; but we must also concede the name of a painting to an outline drawn without any colour at all, and composed merely of shadow and light. For in such designs we see a resemblance, we see form and expression, and modesty, and bravery, although they are altogether devoid of colour; and neither blood is represented, nor the colour of a man's hair or beard; nevertheless these compositions in monochrome are likenesses of people either tawny or white, and even if we drew one of these Indians with a white pencil, yet he would seem black, for there would be his flat nose, and his stiff curling locks and prominent jaw, and a certain gleam about his eyes, to give a black look to the picture and depict an Indian to the eyes of all those who have intelligence. And for this reason I should say that those who look at works of painting and drawing require a mimetic faculty, for no one could appreciate or admire a picture of a horse or of a bull, unless he had formed an idea of the creature represented.''

(II, 22)

TO not like painting is to scorn reality itself, it is to scorn that type of merit we find in poets, because painting, like poetry, delights in representing the traits and actions of heroes for us; it is also to have no regard for the science of proportions, by which art is put at the service even of reason. If we wanted to speak artfully, we could say that painting is an invention of the gods; think of the different aspects of the earth where the meadows are as if painted by the Seasons, and of everything we see in the sky. But to return seriously to the origin of art, imitation is among the oldest of inventions, the same age as nature itself. We owe its discovery to skilled men, who sometimes called it painting and sometimes plastic art. Plastic art itself is divided into several kinds: because to represent in brass, polish Lychnites or Parian marble,[1] or work ivory belongs to the plastic arts, as does the art of engraving on metals. Painting consists of the use of colors, but not of that alone, or rather, it draws more on that unique medium than does another art form from more numerous resources. Indeed, it represents shadows and varies facial expressions [with color], accordingly showing us anger, sorrow, or joy. The plastic arts do not have the means to give eyes their proper spark; they are bright, they are blue-green or dark in the representations in paint. Hair is a blond that is tawny, flaming, golden. Everything has its color—clothing, weapons, houses and rooms, woods, mountains, streams, and the air that surrounds all things. Many artists have excelled in this art; many cities, many kings have loved it passionately . . . .

## PLINY THE ELDER

### *Natural History*

*The techniques of ancient painting*

FOUR colours only were used by the illustrious painters Apelles, Aetion, Melanthius and Nicomachus to execute their immortal works—of whites, Melinum; of yellow ochres, Attic; of reds, Pontic Sinopis; of blacks, atramentum—although their pictures each sold for the wealth of a whole town. (XXXV, 32)

SOME colours are sombre and some brilliant, the difference being due to the nature of the substances or to their mixture. The brilliant colours, which the patron supplies at his own expense to the painter, are cinnabar, Armenium, dragon's blood, gold-solder, indigo, bright purple; the rest are sombre. Of the whole list some are natural colours and some artificial. Natural colours are sinopis, ruddle, Paraetonium, Melinum, Eretrian earth and orpiment; all the rest are artificial, and first of all those which we specified among minerals, and moreover among the commoner kinds yellow ochre, burnt lead acetate, realgar, sandyx, Syrian colour and black.

(XXXV, 77)

IN early days there were two kinds of encaustic painting, with wax and on ivory with a graver or *cestrum* (that is a small pointed graver); but later the practice came in of decorating battleships. This added a third method, that of employing a brush, when wax has been melted by fire; this process of painting ships is not spoilt by the action of the sun nor by salt water or winds. (XXXV, 49)

A surface painted with cinnabar is damaged by the action of sunlight and moonlight. The way to prevent this is to let the wall dry and then to coat it with Punic wax melted with olive oil and applied by means of brushes of bristles while it is still hot, and then this wax coating must be again heated by bringing near to it burning charcoal made of plant-galls, till it exudes drops of perspiration, and afterwards smoothed down with waxed rollers and then with clean linen cloths, in the way in which marble is given a shine. (XXXIII, 40)

PAINTERS using it [the dark purple of Pozzuoli] put a coat of sandyx underneath and then add a coat of dark purple mixed with egg, and so produce the brilliance of cinnabar; if they wish instead to produce the glow of purple, they lay a coat of blue underneath, and then cover this with dark purple mixed with egg. (XXXV, 26)

WHITE earth of Chios . . . dissolved in milk . . . is used for touching up the whitewash on plastered walls. (XXXV, 56)

ALSO a gum exudes from the sarcocolla—that is the name of the tree and also of the gum—which is extremely useful both to painters and to medical men; it resembles incense dust, and for the purposes mentioned the white kind is better than the red; . . . . (XIII, 20)

THE finest glue is made from the ears and genitals of bulls . . . but it is more adulterated than any other, a decoction being made from any old skins and even from shoes. The most reliable glue comes from Rhodes, which is used by painters and physicians. (XXVIII, 236)

THE preparation of all black is completed by exposure to the sun, black for writing ink receiving an admixture of gum and black for painting walls an admixture of glue. Black pigment that has been dissolved in vinegar is difficult to wash out. (XXXV, 25)

WAX becomes dark with the addition of paper ash, and red with an admixture of alkanet; by paints it is made to assume various colours for forming likenesses, for the innumerable uses of men, and even for the protection of walls and of weapons. (XXI, 49)

## LUCIAN

SEEING a huge, magnificent house, lighted up throughout, shining with gold and flowering with paintings, would it be possible not to want to describe it? The educated man who contemplates beautiful things is not content with the enjoyment his eyes have; he does not stand as a mute spectator before these beauties; he tries his best to assimilate them and speak of them in grateful terms . . . . See the difficulty of the attempt—to reconstruct such pictures without colors, without figures, away from the place itself; for words are poor tools to paint with. (*De Æco.,* 1)

## VITRUVIUS

### *Of Architecture*

*On Stucco*

WHEN the walls have been made solid with three coats of sand and also of marble, they will not be subject to cracks or any other fault. But when the hardness has been tested by rapping them for some time with a *baculi,*[2] and when the polishing has given them the shining whiteness of the marble, then the walls, receiving color at the same time as polish, can project the most brilliant glow.

AS for the colors, when they have been carefully laid onto the still moist plaster, they will not come off, but are fixed for good; and that [is] because the lime, deprived of its water in the ovens, empty and porous, absorbs everything it happens to come in contact with, as if constrained by the necessity to feed itself; and by consolidation, taking the source or principle of other elements to itself, it becomes solid in all its parts. As soon as it is dry, it is reconstituted to the point of seeming to have these qualities by nature.

Stucco, therefore, when it is well made does not become rough, and, when it is cleaned, its colors do not wipe off unless they have been applied with little care or on an already dry surface.

Thus, when facings for painting have been laid on as described above, they will remain firm and glowing and strong to a ripe old age. (VII, 3, 6-8)

*On the preparation of minium*

AND so when it [vermilion] is used in the finishing of enclosed apartments, it remains of its own colour without defects; but in open places like peristyles and exedrae and so forth, where the sun and moon can send their brightness and their rays, the part so affected is damaged and becomes black, when the colour loses its strength. (VII, 9, 2)

*On artificial colours*

In the same way they [the stucco painters] prepare whortleberries and mix them with milk, thus making a fine purple. (VII, 14, 3)

*On black*

[SOOT] is then collected and in part compounded with gum and worked up for the use of writing ink; the rest is mixed with size and used by fresco-painters for colouring walls. But if this cannot be obtained, we must satisfy our requirements without holding back the works by the delay involved. Brushwood or pine-chips must be burnt, and when they are charred they are to be pounded in a mortar with size. Thus the fresco-painters will have a not unpleasant black colour. (VII, 10, 2-3)

*On wall-painting*

. . . THE ancients who first used polished stucco began by imitating the variety and arrangement of marble inlay; then the varied distribution of festoons, ferns, coloured strips.

Then they proceeded to imitate the contours of buildings, the outstanding projections of columns and gables; in open spaces, like exedrae, they designed scenery on a large scale in tragic, comic, or satyric style;[2] in covered promenades, because of the length of the walls, they used for ornament the varieties of landscape gardening, finding subjects in the characteristics of particular places. (VII, 5, 1-2)

## PLUTARCH

IT seems as if sight paints all the fantasies that appear to it on a damp surface, so quickly do they fade and disappear from the mind; but the images of those one loves are imprinted on it like figures painted in encaustic and fired, for they leave forms in the memory which move and live and speak and remain forever. (*Anat.*, 16, 759c)

## EUSEBIUS OF CAESAREA

IN executing human figures, sometimes with the bright colors of encaustic, mingled with light and shadow, and sometimes with forms sculptured out of a lifeless material, men try to assure eternal remembrance for the virtues of those they honor. (*Vita Const.*, I, 3)

## BOETHIUS

WHAT constitute the materials of painting are planks of wood trimmed by the hand of a carpenter and covered with a thick coating of wax, glazes for colors zealously hunted by merchants, canvases made by laborious weaving.

## AUSONIUS

IN adding the gloss of your corrections to that sketch, you might give it a wipe with the sponge to achieve the imperfect image of a horse whose sweat froths badly.

(*Carm.*, XXVI, 1, 17–19)

# *The Middle Ages*

IT IS NOT ST. LUKE ALONE WHO IS BLESSED,
BUT ALL THOSE WHO REPRESENT AND WORK TO DEPICT MIRACLES,
THE SACRED PORTRAITS OF OUR LORD AND THE MOTHER OF GOD
AND THE OTHER SAINTS; FOR THIS ART OF PAINTING
IS AGREEABLE TO GOD AND WELL REGARDED BY HIM.

*Dionysius of Phourna of Agrapha*

# DIONYSIUS OF PHOURNA OF AGRAPHA

THE GUIDE TO PAINTING *written by Dionysius, a monk of Phourna, near Agrapha, which the reader finds here under the heading of the Middle Ages, actually belongs to a later century. But its placement is appropriate because of the profoundly traditional character of the ideas and prescriptions it contains. In this connection, it treats of the whole of Byzantine painting since its beginnings. We have omitted the large part of this work devoted to questions of iconography, and publish here the sections that touch on the spirit of that art, full of mystical luxuriance, and some of the numerous prescriptions Dionysius gives us. These rules are hard to apply in our day; industry has displaced them. We think nonetheless that it is a good idea to use them to show the relationship between the painter and his materials in the Byzantine world. It is interesting to imagine the artists of that time, dominated by a theology and a metaphysics but also faced with concrete and natural materials they had to harness, with skill and ingenuity, to the task of exalting the personages of the Christian pantheon.*

## *The Guide to Painting*

TO MARY, MOTHER OF GOD AND EVER VIRGIN

O you who are as splendid as the sun, most beloved and all-gracious Mother of God, Mary! St. Luke, source of eloquence, wisest of physicians, perfect master and accomplished doctor in all sciences and in all fields of knowledge, having been sanctified by the Gospel precepts he preached in a loud voice and wrote, desired to show the whole world clearly the holy love that he had for your gracious and divine grandeur; he judged, and rightly, that there was nothing in his science and spiritual riches that would constitute a worthy offering to you except a representation of your beauty, so admirable and full of grace, which he had actually contemplated with his own eyes. This holy and wise person used all the riches of colors and gold mosaics [1] to paint and impress that image faithfully in pictures drawn according to the rules of his art. I, in turn, have devoted myself to sacred painting, with the hope that my means will not prove inferior to my good will, in order to fulfill my duty toward your holy self, your venerable grandeur and your awesome magnificence.[2] But I confess that I have overreached myself in this difficult task, for my capabilities and means have not kept pace with my intentions. Nevertheless, I have not wanted to abandon this fine plan entirely, or to lose all the fruits of my labors, and I have dared to offer you and put in your hands the exposition and interpretation of that art to which I have applied myself with the greatest care and the most minute attention in order to develop the most suitable method. For I fully appreciate, O Virgin, that you and the Creator of all things deign to look favorably on all that man can do. I therefore present to you this work, which is intended for painters endowed with natural gifts, to help them in the beginnings of this art, and above all to describe good methods, how to use colors, and what subjects to choose. I show how and in what corners of places of worship they must be distributed for the walls to be decorated in a fitting and attractive way by their paintings. I desire above all that your radiant and gracious image be constantly reflected in the mirror of souls and keep them pure until the end of time; that it uplift those who are inclined toward the world; and that it give hope to those who meditate on and imitate that eternal model of beauty. And may I myself, through the assistance of your holy merit, achieve the joy of contemplating you face to face!

## TO ALL PAINTERS, AND TO ALL THOSE WHO, SEEKING INSTRUCTION, READ THIS BOOK, GREETINGS, IN OUR LORD

KNOWING, O industrious disciples of painting, that Our Lord in his holy Gospel censured the man who had hidden his talent, saying to him, "Wicked and lazy servant, you should have used the money I left with you so that on my return I might have received it back with a profit."[3] I myself fear incurring this censure. I have thus not wanted to hide my talent, that is, the little art that I know, that I have learned since my childhood and studied with great effort, trying to imitate as closely as possible the renowned and illustrious master Manuel Panselinos of Thessalonica.[4] After having worked in the admirable churches on the holy mountain of Athos, ornamenting them with magnificent paintings, this painter radiated so brilliant a light by his knowledge in his art that he was compared to the moon in all its splendor. He stands head and shoulders above all painters, ancient and modern, as his paintings on walls and on panels still amply prove. All who have even a little talent will understand this very well if they look on and examine this painter's work. I want to propagate this art of painting, that since my childhood has cost me such effort to learn in Thessalonica,[5] for use by those who want equally to devote themselves to that art, and to explain in this work the subjects of measuring, figures, and colors of flesh and ornamentation with great exactness. I want besides to explain natural dimensions, the work specific for each subject, the different preparations of colors, glue, plaster, and gold, and the way to paint on walls with the greatest perfection. I have also indicated how to treat the whole of the Old and New Testaments—the natural events and miracles in the Bible, and at the same time Our Lord's parables; the legends and epigraphs suitable to each prophet; the name and facial traits of the apostles and the principal saints; their martyrdom and a number of their miracles, according to the ecclesiastical calendar. I describe how to paint churches, and I provide other instructions necessary to the art of painting, as can be seen in the table of contents. I have gathered all these materials with much effort and care, assisted by my student, Master Cyril of Chios, who has corrected it all with great attention. Pray for us then, good readers, so that Our Lord will deliver us from the fear of being censured as bad servants.

The most unworthy of painters,

*Dionysius, monk of Phourna of Agrapha*

*Some preliminary exercises and instructions for him who wants to learn the art of painting*

HE who wants to learn the science of painting should begin to approach it, and prepare himself for some time in advance, by repeatedly making simple drawings, without using dimensions, until he has acquired a little experience and has proved he has ability. Then he should address the following prayer to Jesus Christ, before an image of the Mother of God, Virgin of Safe Conduct,[6] while a priest blesses him: "King of Heaven, etc., etc.,'' following this with the hymn to the Virgin,[7] an invitatory,[8] and the verses of the Transfiguration.[9] Then, after making the sign of the cross on his head, [the priest] should say aloud: ''Let us pray to Our Lord: Lord Jesus Christ, our God, you who possess the unlimited divine nature, who took a body under the heart of the Virgin Mary for man's salvation; you who deigned to imprint the sacred image of your immortal visage on a holy cloth, which served to cure the illness of the satrap Abgar [10] and to open his soul to the knowledge of the true God; you who illuminated with your Holy Spirit your divine apostle and evangelist Luke, so that he might represent the beauty of your most pure Mother,[11] who carried you as a tiny infant in her arms, saying, 'The grace of him born of me flows out to all men'; you who are the divine master of all that exists, illuminate and guide my soul, and the heart and mind of your servant (N.); direct his hands so that he may create a worthy and perfect image of you, your most holy Mother, and all the saints, for the glory, the joy, and the embellishment of your holy Church. Forgive the sins of all those who will venerate these images and who, kneeling piously before them, will render honor to the model who is in Heaven. Guard them from every evil influence, and teach them through good counsel. I entreat you, by the intercession of your most holy Mother, the illustrious apostle and evangelist St. Luke, and all the saints. Amen.''

*Invitatory and conclusion*

AFTER prayer,[12] the student should learn thoroughly the proportions and composition of figures; he should sketch a great deal, working continuously, and with the help of God he will become skillful after a time, as experience has shown me with my pupils. To this end have I worked with pleasure on this writing, so that painters, my brothers in Jesus Christ, and all those who will read this book may act for the glory of God. May they pray to God for me! But if some envious or ill-willed person should cast aspersions in any way on my disinterested aim, let him realize that he will wrong only himself; for as one writer said, envy is an evil thing, but at least it has this advantage, that it eats out the eyes and heart of him it possesses. God knows, I have written this work, insofar as it depended on me, to be useful to him who gives himself to this art, who devotes himself to it with the enthusiasm of a zealous disciple, above all to him to wants to master the instructions in this book. To him I address the counsel that follows, with great friendship.

Understand well, O studious pupil, that if you want to devote yourself to this science of painting, you must go find a wise master who will teach it to you quickly, if he directs you as we say. But if you find only a master whose teaching and art are imperfect, try to do as we have done, that is, seek out some of the original work of the master Manuel Panselinos. Work a long time, using it as your model, directing your efforts as we have already indicated, until you succeed in capturing the proportions and compositions of that painter's figures. Then go into churches where he has done paintings and take anthiboles,[13] in the manner described below. Do not begin your work willy-nilly and without reflection, but act on the contrary in the fear of God and with piety in this art, which is a divine thing. Before taking a tracing from either a wall or a panel, be careful to wash the original or prototype well with a very clean sponge to remove all the dirt on it; for if you do not wash it immediately, the dirt will stick, and will not be removable, and thus you will be thought impious and contemptuous of holy images. In fact, according to the great St. Basil, the respect one renders an image, one renders to the prototype, and scorn of an image often leads to scorn of the reality. O my friends, if I give you this little warning and instruction, I do so for love of God and my brothers, and because I fear sin; for in several of the countries I have visited, I have found pictures from which painters had taken tracings. Perhaps they were ignorant, or perhaps they did not fear sin, but these painters left dirt marks on the pictures which I could not remove no matter what I did. But if the picture you want to trace is old, the color faded, the plaster crumbling, and you are afraid it will be weakened by the work of tracing, use the following method. First wash the picture carefully, restore it delicately, put a coat of varnish on it, and then take a tracing; finally, after that, wash it once again, as we have indicated. This, with the help of God, is all I have set myself to tell you, disinterestedly and openly. Now, my dear friend, go forward courageously, without fear of difficulty, but with all the care and perseverance possible, to learn this art perfectly; for it is a divine work that God has taught us, as is evident to everyone for many reasons, and principally because of the existence of the venerable acheirous image [14] with which the Man-God, Jesus Christ, imprinted his sacred features on a cloth, as the exact and divine type of his face, and sent to Edessa to the satrap Abgar. This excellent work was equally acceptable to the holy Mother of God, and well regarded by her, as everyone knows, since she encouraged and blessed the apostle and evangelist St. Luke because of that science, saying to him, "The grace of him I have borne flows out to them because of me." It is not St. Luke alone who is blessed, but all those who represent and work to depict miracles, the sacred portraits of Our Lord and the Mother of God and the other saints; for this art of painting is agreeable to God and well regarded by him. Hence, all who work with care and piety receive graces and benedictions from Heaven. But those whose efforts rise only from love of money,[15] and who abandon care and piety, should reflect well before their death: they should recall fearfully the punishment of him they imitate—Judas, expiating his crime in the torments of Hell's fire, from which we all hope to be ransomed by the merits of the Mother of God, the apostle St. Luke, and all the saints. Amen.

*How to prepare charcoal for drawing*

TAKE a large, sound section of a hazelnut or myrtle trunk, cut it into several logs with a saw, and split these with a hatchet into small sticks, which you cut down further with a knife to give them the form of pencils; put them in a pot, the upper part of which you cover with a cloth, and over this put a good layer of earth. Then light a fire in the oven, and when it is half-kindled, put the pot in the middle of this oven; then the pieces of wood will catch fire also and burn. As soon as you see no more flames, take the pot out of the oven, and cover it with ashes or dry earth. Be careful not to take the wood pieces out of the pot before they are all cool, because if you uncover the pot before thorough cooling, the wood will reignite and burn itself up, and your efforts will be brought to naught.

If you want a quicker preparation, do this. Wrap several

pieces of wood in paper or cloth, and suround them with live coals. These pieces of wood will burn and produce smoke; but be careful to take them out of the coals as soon as the smoke stops; then bury them in cold ashes or earth until they are extinguished, and then you will have finished. This is how painters prepare charcoal for drawing.

*On the preparation of brushes*

WHEN you want to prepare brushes for painting, you must procure some badger tails; you will use the hairs that grow along the edges. Pick out the straight, smooth hairs, and discard those that are bent or that have knots. Cut the former with scissors, and lay them out separately, one by one, on a board. Next, gather them together, wet them with water, press down on the ends with the nails of your left hand; with your right hand, pull them loose by the other end. Prepare them with care, and bind them well with a waxed silk thread; take care not to make the ligature too long. Be sure to steep the quill into which you will fit the brush in water so that the bristles will not come out; for otherwise, you will not succeed. Put all the ends of tails aside; they can be used as large brushes for polishing surfaces.[16]

*On the preparation of glue*

WHEN you want to prepare glue, do this. Take skins tanned with lime; put these in warm water to wet them through; wash and clean them to remove any flesh and impurities; then boil them in clean water in a copper container. Watch for the moment when they begin to boil and start to break up, and put them in a sieve to drain; put them back in the water and take them out to drain again a second and third time, until they have broken up completely. If you do not find any tanned skins, take untanned ones, choosing skins from around the hoofs or ears of a beef and other skins that can serve no other purpose or that have little value. It matters little if these pieces are large; buffalo hide is as good as beef. Then you prepare them as follows. Take quicklime, put it in a bucket, and add water until the lime is well dissolved and diluted; put the skins in, and leave them until the hair falls out of itself—about a week. After that, pull the skins out, and wash and clean them well. Then dry them, and follow the directions above to make glue out of them. But if you are in a hurry or you have no quicklime, begin by soaking the untanned hides, and then boil them a little. Take them out of the pot, scrape away all the grease and flesh, and make cuts in the skins with a knife so they will cook more quickly; do not separate the pieces entirely, but leave them joined, so that they will be easier to drain. Then, by boiling them, you will get glue. If you want to dry the glue, boil it alone on a low heat until it thickens; but keep an eye on it, because it may boil up and spill over. You must therefore be present so that when it sets to boiling, you can lift it off the fire at the moment it begins to boil over. You stop the spilling over by placing the bottom of the container in cold water, which you have set beside you for this purpose. Put the glue back on the fire several times, until it has congealed, and then cool it. Stretching a string taut, use it to cut the glue into small pieces. Put these pieces on a board, and leave them there two or three days, until they begin to harden; then thread them with a cord, and suspend them in the air until they have dried completely. This way, you can keep them and use them as you need. Be sure to prepare glue in cold weather; because if it is warm, the process does not work so well, but the glue spoils easily.

*How to prepare plaster*

WHEN you want to cook and make plaster, do this. First, choose it with care; then break it up into small pieces with a hammer; use only plaster that is quite white and bright. Next, light an oven and get it red hot. Take out the coals. Sweep it well and quickly with a besom, and put the gypsum in the oven, which you keep from cooling by carefully covering it and putting over it a layer of dampened earth that you have prepared in advance and have ready at hand. Watch to see that the earth develops no cracks until it is quite dry, because this would let heat escape; to avoid this inconvenience, everything must be hermetically sealed. Three days later, take the plaster out of the oven. If it is well cooked, so much the better; if it is not cooked enough, you will just have a little more trouble powdering it. When you have taken it out of the oven, pound it out on a stone and pass it through a very fine sieve; pound what remains in the sieve, and sift it again, until it is all quite fine. Next, prepare your plaster in the following manner. Warm water in a copper container, and be sure to have cold and warm water beside you, because you must work the gypsum in water that is neither too warm nor too cool. Dip your hands into the water and swirl it around, so that the plaster does not stick to the sides of the container. Someone else will pour the plaster very slowly, little by little, into the water, while you take care to stir it up and mix it well so that it forms neither large nor small lumps. If you let lumps form, they will turn as hard as rocks and you will not be able to pulverize them. Be careful also not to put a lot of plaster in a copper container, because when the container has little water in it, the gypsum sticks to its sides and becomes as hard as stone, which means you will not be able to remove it without destroying the container. In fifty eggshellsful of water, put no more than twenty eggshellsful of gypsum, or even less, if you want, but not more. In other words, to prepare good plaster, you must put a small quantity of it in a pot containing a lot of water. After this, let the powder filter down to the bottom of the container, from which you then remove the water little by little, until the plaster remains as if coagulated; then take it out of the pot, spread it out on boards, and let it dry completely. If you are in a hurry, drain it in a cloth, which will be quickly done, and then spread it out on boards, as we have indicated. When it is quite dry, heat the oven a second time, and bake the plaster again. Powder and prepare it as the first time, and dry it on boards. Or, to speed the process up, put the plaster in a warm oven, or expose it to the sun, which will not spoil it, but on the contrary will improve it. Finally, you powder it fine and put it away, to mix with glue and make plaster coatings of it as you wish.[17] . . .

*How to gild images*

DRAW an image with a very fine point; then clean the picture well, and remove any spots it may have by scratching carefully. Next, put two or three coats of ampoli [18] on the picture. When these coats are dry, lay the picture down flat. Take pieces of gold leaf and apply them to the drawing, fixing the edges of each leaf with a bone instrument so that they will not blow off. Next, put some raki [19] in a small pot with a spout, and pour the liquor on the edges of the picture. Then pick up the picture and tilt it to make the raki run over it and impregnate the whole surface. Be sure to do this quickly so that the plaster does not dry. Set the picture up again, patch any small defects, let it dry, and lastly burnish it. . . .

*How to make flesh color (from Panselinos)*

TAKE some Venetian or good French rouge,[20] in cakes, . . . drams; some Venetian ocher, . . . drams (or another if you cannot get this); and some cinnabar [vermilion], . . . drams. If you want this color to be richer, begin by powdering the cinnabar; precipitate it in some water, draw the water off, and use only the deposit that forms at the bottom. You will get a very fine color this way.[21]

*On reds*

FOR the face of the holy Virgin and young saints, you must put a very light layer of rouge on the middle of the countenance, being very careful to blend the cinnabar with the flesh color. In the shadows and on the contours of the hands, you must apply a very thin layer of bole, as also to make the wrinkles on old people. The parts above the eyes should be separated with glycasm,[22] as we said above.

*On hair and beards*

TAKE some dark ocher; heat it over a flame until it becomes a dark red, and when you want to paint the hair of Christ or young saints, add a little black and grind them together. Next take a little egg white and some black, and make some light umber. For very dark umbers, use pure egg white: some black and ocher for the first layer; for the second, pure ocher, which you must be careful to blend carefully on the edges. To make saints' lips, mix some rouge and some cinnabar; for the mouths, use only cinnabar; for the opening of the mouth, mix cinnabar with other colors. In areas almost completely lacking in light, use some black and some umber; for eyebrows, first put on some fine glycasm, which you touch up with a few highlights. This is how to do the hair, lips, mouths, and eyebrows of young saints. But paint the beards and hair of old people thus. Add some rouge and a little black to some egg white, and lay on a first coat; next, put a second, lighter layer on the light areas, and add some black on the shadows. To set off beards, highlight them with a little rouge; this will make them more lustrous. Do the same with mustaches, and use pure bole by itself for the mouths. On the lips, put a little red flesh color; on the eyebrows, you can put some glycasm, or you can leave it off. This is how to paint the hair, beards, and lips of old people.

*On making ink*

TAKE an eggshellful of apple-tree bark; put it in a container with about one and a half eggshellsful of water. Let the bark soak a week or two, exposing it to the sun if you want. Grind ten drams of gallnuts and fifteen drams of calacanthi.[23] Put them all together in a pot or copper container, and cook the mixture until it is reduced by half. Filter it in a fine cloth, and wash the residue with ten drams of water, which you put in the melagni.[24] Filter it again in a fine cloth. Put the pure ink back in the first pot you cooked in. Grind up ten drams of very pure gum; throw it into the liquid, and put the pot on the fire until the gum has melted. It would be better, though, to melt it without heat. Keep this ink in glass, and write when you want, because this ink is very good. . . .

*Notes on the proportions of the human body*

ON the facing page, draw the body of a man and his limbs.

Learn, O my student, that a man's body is nine heads[25] tall, that is, nine head-lengths from the forehead to the heels. Make the first length so as to divide it into three parts: the forehead for the first, the nose for the second, and the beard for the third. Make the hair the length of a nose, apart from the measure of the head. Subdivide the space between the beard and the nose into three parts; the chin is two parts, the mouth is one, and the throat equals a nose-length. Next, from the chin to the middle of the body, there are three head-lengths; to the knees, two more. There is a nose-length for the knee; from the knees to the anklebones, two more head-lengths; then from the anklebone to the heels, a nose-length. From there to the toenails, a head-length. From the larynx to the shoulder, a head-length also; the same to the other shoulder. For the round of the shoulder, one head-length; from the elbow to the wristbone, a head-length; from the wrists to the fingernails, a head-length. A head-length also to the tips of the fingers. The two eyes are equal to each other, and the space between them equals one eye. When the head is in profile, make the distance between the eye and the ear the measure of two eyes; if the head is full face, make it only one eye-measure. The ear should be equal to the nose. When the figure is naked, four nose-lengths are needed for half his width; when he is clothed, the width of his chest is a head-length and a half; the belt must be raised to the level of the elbows.[26]

*On the preparation of colors, and how to paint with oil on cloth*

FIRST, grind the colors well in water, and let them dry completely. Grind them a second time with uncooked peseri, and heap the mixture up on the stone to put it in a saucer. When you want to work, you lift the skin that has formed on the surface to get at your color. For rouge, the best procedure is to grind it with nut oil. Now, nail four pieces of wood together, and stretch cloth over this frame. If the material you use is silk, you can draw on it directly and begin to work; but if it is linen or another kind of cloth, you must begin by laying a thick coating of gesso on it, which you spread on with a brush and let dry. Next, you draw on it with chalk, and then you begin to work. You take a small board in the shape of a palette, and on it you can mix your colors and thin them with naphtha. Begin by painting the shadows, and paint the lighter and lighter areas successively, finishing by using your white. Try not to put one coat on another; but lay the coats on adroitly, each where it belongs; otherwise they will not dry without staining. Do the same with flesh, that is, begin with the shadows and end with the highlights. When you work, lean your painting back, and on finishing, give it a coat of varnish. You must have a brush for each color, and these brushes must be long and firm. You must have a good many boxes in your cupboard to lay your brushes out in, protected from dust. When you want to wash them, take a tin can divided into two sections. In one, put some uncooked peseri; [27] you put a little in your hand to soften the brushes in. When the paint is soft, you press it out in the other section and then scrape up this residue, which can be used again to paint with.[28] Then wash the brushes with soap or in [a solution of] a little nitric acid: this cleans them perfectly well, as it does the grinding stone. There are our instructions for preparing and using oil paints.

*Guide to painting on walls, that is, how to paint*

HOLD in mind that the brushes to use for outlining should be made of hair from an ass's mane or an ox's dewlap, the stiff hair of a goat, or a mule's whiskers. You make them by tying *on walls and prepare the brushes destined for that use*

these hairs together and fastening them to an eagle quill. They can be used to outline, to paint flesh and light areas, or for other things. For varnish brushes, you must use pig hairs; you first bind them together with wax, and then you attach them to a wooden shaft, without using quills.

*How to plaster walls*

WHEN you want to paint a church, you must begin with the highest points and finish at the lowest. For this reason, you begin by putting up a ladder. Next, take water in a large container and throw spoonsful of it on the wall in order to wet it. If this wall is made of earth, scratch the earth with a trowel as deeply as you can, because [otherwise] the lime plaster would slake off later, particularly from the vault. Wet the surface again and smooth it. If the wall is brick, you wet it down five or six times, and you lay on a coating of lime plaster two fingers thick or more to hold moisture and to give yourself a proper working surface. If the wall is stone, wet it only once or twice, and lay on a much thinner amount of plaster, for the stone takes moisture easily and does not dry out. In winter, lay a coat on in the evening and another, thinner one the next morning. In good weather, do what best suits your needs, and, after laying on the last coat, smooth it quite level; let it become firm, and work.

*How to draw when working on walls*

WHEN you are going to draw on a wall, first smooth and level its surface well. Then take a compass, and attach a wooden stick to each leg so that you can spread them as wide as you want. Attach a brush to the end of one of these sticks. You describe the halos of your figures, and you indicate all the necessary measurements. Next, make a very light sketch with ocher; complete your outlines. If you want to erase something, use oxy.[29] Work over the halos, polish the surface thoroughly, and use your black; polish the garments and coat then with egg white. Try to finish what you are going to polish very quickly; for if you delay too long, a crust will form on the surface which will not absorb the color. Work the faces the same way; you make the outlines with a bone shaped to a point, and lay the flesh tint on as quickly as possible, before a crust forms, as we said above . . . .[30]

# THEOPHILUS

THE MONK THEOPHILUS *lived in the twelfth century. For a time he was identified with a Benedictine monk named Roger, a goldsmith at the monastery of Helmarshausen in Westphalia. This theory has today been abandoned, and there is a tendency to reject the notion that Theophilus was a creator. As a matter of fact, he no less proved to be an informed collector of theories and practices current in his time and revelatory of Greek art as well as Italian, French as well as German, and even Arabian. As a result, his* Schedula diversarum artium *is the primary contemporary source of information on painting in the Middle Ages. The reader will find in the following pages the chapter specifically devoted to that subject. Theophilus' work is composed of a collection of directions on how to procure various coloring agents, how to apply them to the painting surface, how to make glue and varnish, and so forth. There is nothing here that is not concrete, and the instructions are purely technical; but today, apart from the historic interest of this reading, a new value attaches to Theophilus' work: poetry. It is surprising and intriguing to see certain materials, objects, and substances appear in these pages devoted to what our painters would call shoptalk that the present-day artist no longer needs or wants but that make us dream: ground hartshorn, horsetail gathered in the summer and dried in the sun, beaver or bear or wild boar teeth, hammer cast from aurichalcum,[1] rotted sticks cut in April, old or beer-laced wine, cherry- or plum-tree gum, tortoiseshell or seashells, fish bladder, aged white of egg, gold dust amalgamated with mercury and filtered through deerskin, glass pearls, bull gall and coarse salt, flower of brass, iris or leek juice, ground hawthorn, and so on. This delightful alchemy deserved to be included here.*

## *The Various Arts*

*Prologue*

THE processes of the various arts are learned gradually. To paint, first learn how to make up colors; then apply yourself with care to mixing them well. Practice your work, and bring the greatest precision to everything; your paintings should be ornamented without sacrificing the natural; then, the many teachings of the masters will lay open the domain of art: this book will furnish the proof.

*Preface to the first book*

THEOPHILUS—humble priest, servant of the servants of God, unworthy of the name and profession of monk—wishes to all, who are willing to avoid and spurn idleness and the shiftlessness of the mind by the useful occupation of their hands and the agreeable contemplation of new things, the recompense of a heavenly reward!

In the account of the creation of the world, we read that man was created in the image and likeness of God and was animated by the Divine breath, breathed into him. By the eminence of such distinction, he was placed above the other living creatures, so that, capable of reason, he acquired participation in the wisdom and skill of the Divine Intelligence, and, endowed with free will, was subject only to the will of his Creator, and revered His sovereignty. Wretchedly deceived by the guile of the Devil, through the sin of disobedience he lost the privilege of immortality, but, however, so far transmitted to later posterity the distinction of wisdom and intelligence, that whoever will contribute both care and concern is able to attain a capacity for all arts and skills, as if by hereditary right.

Human skill sustained this purpose and, in its various activities, pursued profit and pleasure and, finally, with the passage of time transmitted it to the predestined age of Christian religion. So, it has come about that, what God intended to create for the praise and glory of His name, a people devoted to God has restored to His worship.

Therefore, let not the pious devotion of the faithful neglect what the wise foresight of our predecessors has transmitted to our age; what God has given man as an inheritance, let man strive and work with all eagerness to attain. When this has been attained, let no one glorify himself, as if it were received of himself and not Another, but let him humbly render thanks to God, from Whom and through Whom all things are, and without Whom nothing is. Nor let him conceal what has been given in the cloak of envy, or hide it in the closet of a grasping heart. But, repelling all vain-glory, let him with a joyful heart and with simplicity dispense to all who seek, in fear of the Gospel judgment on that merchant who failed to restore to his master his talent with added interest, and, deprived of all reward, merited the censure from his master's lips of being a wicked servant.[2]

Fearful of incurring this judgment, I, an unworthy and frail mortal of little consequence, freely offer to all, who wish to learn with humility, what has freely been given me by the Divine condescension, which gives to all in abundance and holds it against no man. I exhort them to recognise God's favour towards me and to appreciate His generosity, and I would have them know that they can be quite sure that the same things are at hand for themselves if they will add their own labour. For, as it is wicked and detestable for man in any way to strive after, or take by theft, what is forbidden or not intended for him, so, to fail to strive after what is rightfully his and an inheritance from God the Father, or to hold it in contempt, must be put down to laziness and foolishness.

Therefore, dearest son—whoever you may be, whose heart is inspired by God to investigate the vast field of the various arts and apply your mind and care in order to gather from it what pleases you—do not despise useful and precious things, simply because your native earth has produced them for you of its own accord or unexpectedly. For, foolish is the merchant who suddenly finds a treasure in a hole in the ground and fails to pick it up and keep it. If the common vines were to produce myrrh, frankincense and balsam for you: if your native springs were to pour forth oil, milk and honey: if, instead of nettles and thistles and other weeds of the garden, nard, calamus and various spices grew, surely you would not still despise them as mean and homely, and voyage over lands and seas to procure foreign things, not better but probably more mean. This, you would consider to be great folly. For, however much men are accustomed to place in the first rank precious things that are sought with much toil and acquired at great expense, and to look after them with great solicitude, yet, if meanwhile they happen to find or come across things for nothing that are comparable or better, then they keep these with a similar, even greater care.

Wherefore, dearest son,—whom God has made wholly

happy in this regard, in so far as those things are offered freely, for which many at the greatest peril of life plough the sea waves compelled to endure hunger and cold, or which others, wearied with long servitude in the schools and not exhausted by the desire of learning, only acquire with intolerable labour—be eager and anxious to look at this little work on the various arts, read it through with a retentive memory, and cherish it with a warm affection. If you will diligently examine it, you will find in it whatever kinds and blends of various colours Greece possesses: whatever Russia knows of workmanship in enamels or variety of niello: whatever Arabia adorns with repoussé or cast work, or engravings in relief: whatever gold embellishments Italy applies to various vessels or to the carving of gems and ivories: whatever France esteems in her precious variety of windows: whatever skilled Germany praises in subtle work in gold, silver, copper, iron, wood and stone.

When you have read through these things several times and commended them to a retentive memory, you will recompense me for the labour of instruction if every time you make good use of my work you pray to Almighty God to have mercy on me. He knows that I have written the things collected here out of no love for human approbation nor greed for temporal gain, and that I have not appropriated anything precious or rare nor kept silent about something reserved especially for myself from malice or envy, but that, to increase the honour and glory of His name, I have ministered to the necessities of the many and had regard to their advantage.

*The mixing of colours for nude bodies*

THE colour, which is called the flesh tone, with which the face and nude bodies are painted is composed as follows. Take flake-white—which is white made from lead—and, without grinding it, put it just as it is, dry, in a copper or iron pot, place it over a fire and heat it until it has changed to a yellow colour. Then grind it and mix with it some ordinary flake-white and vermilion until it becomes the colour of flesh. Mix these colours according to how you want them: for example, if you want to have red faces add more vermilion; if you want light faces add more white, and, if pallid ones, add instead of vermilion a little green earth.

*The colour, green earth*

GREEN earth is a pigment, which looks like viridian mixed with black. Its nature is such that it is not ground upon stone, but, when put in water, it dissolves and is then carefully strained through a cloth. On a new wall it can be very usefully employed as a green colour.

*The first shadow colour for flesh*

WHEN you have mixed the flesh colour and with it filled in the faces and nude [parts of] figures, mix with it green earth and red (which is burnt from ochre) and a little vermilion, and prepare the shadow colour for flesh. With this you define the eyebrows and eyes, the nostrils and mouth, the chin, the hollows round the nostrils and the temples, the lines of the forehead and neck, the curves of the face, the beards of young men, the relief of the hands and feet, and all the parts that are separately defined in the nude figure.

*The first rose colour*

THEN mix with the plain flesh colour a little vermilion and a little red lead and prepare the colour which is called rose. With this you redden the upper and lower jaw, the mouth and lower chin, the neck, the wrinkles of the forehead slightly, the forehead itself on each side above the temple, the length of the nose, on each side above the nostrils, and the relief of the other nude parts of the figure.

*The first highlight*

AFTER this, with the plain flesh colour mix ground flake-white and prepare the colour which is called the highlight. With this you will paint the eyebrows, the length of the nose, on each side above the openings of the nostrils, the fine lines around the eyes, below the temples, above the chin, near the nostrils and on each side of the mouth, the upper forehead, between the wrinkles of the forehead—sparingly, the neck in the middle, around the ears, around the relief of the hands and feet and the centre of the highest relief of the hands, feet and arms.

*The dark grey which is applied to the eyes*

THEN mix black with a little white; this colour is called dark grey. With it fill in the pupils of the eyes. Add to it still more white and fill the eyes on either side. Between this colour and the pupil apply plain white and blend in with water.

*The panels of altars and doors and casein glue*

THE panels of altars or doors are first carefully joined together one by one with the cramp which coopers and barrelmakers use. Then they are stuck together with casein glue, which is made in this way.

Soft cheese is cut up into small pieces and washed in warm water with a pestle and mortar until the water, which you have poured on several times, comes out unclouded. Then this cheese is thinned out by hand and placed in cold water until it becomes hard. After this it is broken up finely on a smooth wooden board with a piece of wood. It is then replaced in the mortar and carefuly pounded with the pestle, and water mixed with quicklime is added until it becomes as thick as lees. With this glue the panels are fastened together. When they have dried, they stick together so firmly that they cannot be separated by damp or heat.

Later, they should be levelled with an iron spokeshave which is curved and has an edge on the inner side and two handles so that it can be used with both hands. With this, panels, doors and shields are planed down until they are perfectly smooth. These are covered with the untanned hide of a horse, an ass or a cow, which has been soaked in water until the hairs can be scraped off; then some of the water is wrung out and, while still damp, it is stuck on with the casein glue.

*Whitening hide and wood with gesso*

AFTER this take some gypsum burnt like lime, or the chalk used for whitening skins, and carefully grind it on a stone with water. Then put it in an earthenware pot, pour in some of the hide-glue and place it over a fire until the glue melts. Then spread this very thinly over the hide with a paintbrush, and, when it is dry, spread it rather more thickly and, if necessary, apply a third coat. When it is completely dry, take the plant called shaveweed, which grows like a bulrush and is knotty. You gather it in the summer, dry it in the sun, and rub this whitening with it until it is completely smooth and shining. If you do not have any leather to cover the panels with, cover them in the same way with new linen or hemp cloth of medium strength, using the same glue.

*Sticky varnish*

PUT some linseed oil in a small new pot and add some finely powdered gum called sandarac. This looks like very clear incense, but when broken up has a brighter glitter. When you have placed it over a fire, heat it carefully, without letting it boil, until a third part has evaporated, and be careful of the flame because it is extremely dangerous and is difficult to extinguish if it catches fire. Every painting coated with this varnish becomes bright and decorative and completely durable.

*Grinding colours with oil and gum*

ALL kinds of colours can be ground with this [linseed] oil and used on woodwork—but only on objects which can be dried in the sun, because each time that you apply a colour, you cannot apply another over it until the first has dried. On figures this is a particularly long and tedious process.

If, however, you want to speed up your work, take the gum which oozes from the cheery or plum tree, cut it up very small, and place in an earthenware pot. Pour in plenty of water, and place it in the sun, or in winter over a fire, until the gum melts, and stir carefully with a round piece of wood. Then strain it through a cloth and, with this [drying] medium, grind the colours and apply them. All colours and their combinations can be ground and used with this medium, except red lead, flake-white and vermilion, which are ground up and applied with the white of egg. Spanish green is not mixed with sap green when it is to be coated with varnish, but it can be applied by itself with the medium. You can, however, mix it with other colours if you wish.

*How many times the same colour may be applied*

YOU ought to apply all colours on wood three times, whether ground with oil or the [drying] medium. When the painting is completed and dried and the work has been carried out into the sun, carefully spread over it the sticky varnish, and when this begins to run with the heat, rub it gently with the hand. Do this three times and then leave it until it is thoroughly dried.

*The translucent painting*

A painting, which is called translucent, is also made on wood and by some it is described as lustrous. You make it in this way.

Take some tinfoil, not coated with varnish nor coloured with saffron but plain just as it is. Polish it carefully, and with it cover the area you want to paint by this method. Then very carefully grind the colours, which are to be applied, with linseed oil. When they are extremely thin, apply them with a paintbrush, and so allow them to dry.

*Vermilion*

IF you wish to make vermilion, take some sulphur of which there are three kinds—white, black and yellow. Break it up on a dry stone, and add to it two parts of quicksilver, weighing them on the scales. When you have carefully mixed them, put them in a glass jar, cover this on every side with clay, stop up the mouth so that no vapour can escape, and put it on a fire to dry. Then place it in a burning fire and, when it begins to get hot, you will soon hear a cracking noise inside caused by the quicksilver combining with the burning sulphur. When the noise has stopped, remove the jar at once, open it and take the colour.

*Salt green*

IF you wish to make a green colour take a piece of oak of whatever length and width you like, and hollow it out in the form of a box. Then take some copper and have it beaten into thin sheets, as wide as you like but long enough to go over the width of the hollow box. After this, take a dish full of salt and, firmly compressing it, put it in the fire and cover it with coal overnight. The next day, very carefully grind it on a dry stone. Next, gather some small twigs, place them in the above-mentioned hollow box so that two parts of the cavity are below and a third above, coat the copper sheets on each side with pure honey over which you sprinkle pounded salt, place them together over the twigs and carefully cover them with another piece of wood, prepared for the purpose, so that no vapour can escape. Next, have an opening bored in a corner of this piece of wood through which you can pour warm vinegar or hot urine until a third part of it is filled, and then stop up the opening. You should put this wooden container in a place where you can cover it on every side with dung. After four weeks take off the cover and whatever you find on the copper scrape off and keep. Replace it again and cover it as above.

*Spanish green*

IF you want to make Spanish green, take some plates of copper that have been beaten thin, carefully scrape them on each side, pour over them pure, warm vinegar, without honey and salt, and put them in a small hollowed out piece of wood in the above way. After two weeks, inspect and scrape them and do this until you have enough colour.

*Flake-white and red lead*

TO prepare flake-white, get some sheets of lead beaten out thin, place them, dry, in a hollow piece of wood, like the copper above, and pour in some warm vinegar or urine to cover them. Then, after a month, take off the cover and remove whatever white there is, and again replace it as at first. When you have a sufficient amount and you wish to make red lead with it, grind this flake-white on a stone without water, then put it in two or three new pots and place it over a burning fire. You have a slender curved iron rod, fitted at one end in a wooden handle and broad at the top, and with this you can stir and mix this flake-white from time to time. You do this for a long time until the red lead becomes completely red.

*Ink*

TO make ink, cut for yourself some wood of the hawthorn—in April or May before they produce blossom or leaves—collect them together in small bundles and allow them to lie in the shade for two, three or four weeks until they are fairly well dried out.

Then have some wooden mallets, and with them pound these thorns on a hard piece of wood until you can completely peel off the bark, which you immediately put in a barrel full of water. When you have filled two, three, four or five barrels with bark and water, allow them to stand like this for eight days until the water has drawn off all the sap of the bark. Then put this water into a very clean pot or into a cauldron, place it on the fire and heat it. From time to time, put some of this bark into the pot so that, if there is any sap left in it, it can be boiled out, and, when you have heated it for a little, take it out and put in some more. This done, boil down what remains of the water to a third [of its original quantity], pour it from this pot into a smaller one and continue to heat it until it becomes black and begins to thicken, taking particular care that you do not add any water except that which was mixed with the sap. When you see it become thick, add a third part of pure wine, put it in two or three new pots and continue to heat it until you see that it develops a kind of skin at the top.

Then lift these pots off the fire and put them in the sun until the black ink resolves itself from the red dregs. Afterwards, take some small, carefully sewn, parchment bags like bladders, pour the pure ink into them and hang them up in the sun until it is completely dried. When it is dried, take from it as much as you want, mix it with wine over a fire, add a little iron vitriol and write. If, as a result of carelessness, the ink is not black enough, take a piece of iron, an inch thick, put it on the fire until it is red hot and then throw it into the ink.

# CENNINO CENNINI

CENNINO CENNINI *was born at Colle di Valdesa in the 1360s. He was a student of Agnolo Gaddi, whose father, Taddeo Gaddi, was himself an assistant of Giotto's. We can consider, then, that the teachings Cennini has passed on to us come from the atelier of the great Tuscan master. His* Book of Art, or Treatise on Painting *is the most complete treatment there is of the painting of the late Middle Ages. It should thus be placed after the more "primitive" treatise of Theophilus. It informs us about the theory and practice of drawing, color, fresco, illuminating, oil and tempera painting, gilding, varnishing or glazing, and so forth. Cennini finished drafting his book July 31, 1437, at an advanced age, incarcerated in a prison called Delle Stinche in Florence because of some unpaid debt. We have selected for our readers the passages in this work where he discusses specifically drawing, fresco work, and panel painting.*

*We should note that though Cennini still belongs to the Middle Ages because of his fundamental ideas, we see in him a greater attention to the personality of the painter. He advises his reader first to choose his master according to his own qualities, and then to strike out in pursuit of a personal expression. He goes so far as to eulogize "fantasy." Finally, he recommends the study of nature. He remains nonetheless in the medieval spirit by the dependence he shows on the Church: he invokes the Holy Trinity, the Blessed Virgin, and all the saints in Heaven to lead his work to a successful conclusion. So did Fra Angelico pray before beginning each picture, that he might paint under the guidance and for the glory of the Lord alone.*

## *The Book of Art, or Treatise on Painting*

*Letter-preface by Auguste Renoir*

My dear Mottez,

The republication of Cennino Cennini's *Treatise on Painting* you give us today is above all, to your thinking, a well-deserved homage to the memory of its translator, who was one of the truest and most gifted artists of the past century. You also considered—and you were right—that the public would welcome a new edition of this singular work, presently almost impossible to find in our bookstores.

Singular, I say: Cennini's book deserves more than this epithet. It contains many *lessons on things* that are worth more than the counsels one rarely listens to; moreover, it is illustrated with examples taken from the life of the author's contemporaries, and this gives it the savor of old memories that make us relive another time.

Now, to return to the past is perhaps not useless for the present-day mind. If in fact we must guard against being paralyzed in the forms we have inherited, we must not either try to cut ourselves entirely loose from the centuries that have gone before us out of love of progress. But this is a tendency that many exhibit, and it is quite explainable. So many marvelous discoveries have been made in the last hundred years that men seem to have forgotten in their fascination that others have lived before them. Thus, it is good that a man like Cennini comes to remind them that they have had ancestors they must not disown.

Cennini's treatise is not just a technical manual; it is also a history book that speaks to us not about battles and not about court intrigues, but that initiates us into the life of those elite workers through whom Italy, like Greece and France through theirs, gained the purest glory. If they did not always make a fortune or leave a name behind, they enriched their country with an immeasurable treasure and created for it the physiognomy by which we distinguish it from others. The fact bears repeating that it is the whole of the works left by numbers of forgotten or unknown artists that makes a country's greatness, and not the original work of a man of genius, who, isolated among his contemporaries, most often cannot be contained within borders or times: he exceeds them. The others, on the contrary, personify simultaneously their times and their territory, almost their soil. This said, without intending to slight the glory a Raphael, a Titian, an Ingres, a Corot bequeaths his time, his country, it would be nigh on impossible, wouldn't it, to write a treatise on painting for these exceptional beings. Those the Italian master addressed did not all have genius, but they were nonetheless marvelous workmen.

And to make good artisans is the unique goal Cennini set himself: your father well understood its practical scope. Victor Mottez, one of Ingres' favorite students, had the same admiration as his master for the great productions of schools, true corporate masterpieces that characterized the Italian Renaissance. He knew them well, moreover, and his eyes and his heart were filled with their memory. In a certain way he synthesized his studies and meditations in his beautiful frescoes of Saint-Germain-l'Auxerrois which today have disappeared, irreparably damaged in just a few years by dampness.

I imagine that the artist, who dreamed of restoring the fresco to its former eminence in architectural decoration, felt great joy in translating Cennini's book; it must even have given him encouragement to persevere in his attempts at renovation, undaunted by the disappointments they would bring him.

Your father, who like the poet could have said that he had come too late into a world too old, was the victim of a generous illusion. He believed it was possible to do again what others had done several centuries before our own. He knew that the great decorative ensembles of the Italian masters were the work not of a single man but of a collective, an atelier that the master's spirit animated. He hoped to see a similar collaboration born again to give birth to new masterpieces.

The milieu your father lived in sustained his dream. He belonged in fact to that army of young artists who worked in Ingres' shadow and whose fraternal association had taken on the appearance of the ateliers of earlier days. It was only an appearance, for no one can live outside his time, and ours does not encourage the re-establishment of such intimate congregations.

Cennino Cennini shows us why this is impossible simply by exposing the life of the painters of his time. For them, the glory of accomplishing a beautiful work took the place of payment; they worked to gain Heaven, and not to make their fortune.

Furthermore, in Cennini's time they decorated churches, while today they decorate railroad stations; we must all agree that our contemporaries are less fortunate in the source of their inspiration than their forebears. But above all, there was in play an essential condition for the production of collective works, the condition that gave them unity: painters had the same craft, that craft we shall never know thoroughly because no one can teach it to us any more since we have freed ourselves from our traditions.

This craft of the painters of the Italian Renaissance was also the same as that of their predecessors. If the Greeks had left us a treatise on painting, you can believe it would be identical with Cennini's.

All painting from that of Pompeii, done by the Greeks,[1] to that of Corot by way of Poussin seems to have come from the same palette. Everyone used to learn that way of painting from his master; his genius, if he had any, did the rest.

The apprenticeship of a painter, moreover, did not differ in Cennini's time from that of men in other trades. In the master's atelier they did not just draw; they learned to make brushes, to mix colors, to prepare panels and canvases. Little by little they were initiated into the rigors of the craft, into that formidable skill with colors which only the long experience of generation after generation can teach.

The exacting apprenticeship imposed on young painters never prevented their originality from flowering. Raphael, Perugino's studious assistant, nonetheless became the divine Raphael.

But to explain the general value of early art, we must remember that beyond the master's instructions there lay something else, now also gone, that filled the souls of Cennini's contemporaries: religious feeling, the richest source of their inspiration. This is what gives all their works that noble and at the same time forthright character we find so appealing. In a word, there was in those days a harmony between men and the milieu they moved in, and that harmony came from a common belief. This is understandable, if we realize that the concept of the divine among superior people has always involved ideas of order, hierarchy, and tradition. There is no question here, of course, of an act of faith, but of a simple recognition of fact. It is easy to see that if it is correct to say men conceived celestial society in the image of terrestrial society, then it is even truer that this divine organization in turn had a considerable influence on men's minds and conditioned their ideal. From this we can grasp the cause of the general elevation of art and its unity everywhere that a high religious conception reigns—in Egypt, Greece, Western Europe—so clearly as almost to say that apart from the principles this religious conception contains, there would be no art here.

Men's religious feeling weakened little by little over the centuries, but the rules established under its influence had such solid foundations that until the revolutionary period what remained of them sufficed to sustain art on a high level among people of Catholic culture. I use the expression *Catholic culture* deliberately, because in my opinion it defines the essential difference between the ideas of beauty it calls forth and those evoked by the Christian culture of early, anarchic times, egalitarian and smitten with ugliness. If Christianity had triumphed in its primitive form, we would have had no beautiful cathedrals or sculptures or paintings. Happily, the Egyptian and Greek gods were not all dead; their introduction into the new religion saved beauty from perdition.

Abandoned by the masses, Catholicism seems to many to be in its death throes with nothing on the horizon to replace it. People want no more gods, and gods are necessary to our imagination. We must admit that though modern rationalism can satisfy scientists, it is a mode of thinking incompatible with a conception of art. To tell the truth, this is indeed a religion for certain people, who would designate the gallery of machines (less beautiful by any standards than Notre-Dame) as its temple, but it does not have the requisite qualities to stimulate the sensibilities, if indeed these are not proscribed in the name of reason.[2]

At the time of her greatest power, the Church, which was tyrannical under other circumstances, allowed artists an almost limitless independence. The faith was the governor on their fantasy, which could then quaff fearlessly at profane sources; under the influence of Hellenism, early revived and warmly welcomed in Italy and France, the cult of beauty reappeared in the world, and Catholicism gave it a new face.

The cult of beauty took hold not only in what we call the fine arts; the commonest and most ordinary objects carried its mark. Everyone in those happy times seemed to bring to his work, no matter how humble, the same ambition to attain perfection. The least trifle stands witness to a purity of taste in its maker that we would seek in vain in modern production.

We must note, however, that along with religious feeling other causes contributed largely to endowing the artisan of earlier times with qualities that put him beyond comparison, among them, for example, the rule of having a single workman produce an object from beginning to end. As a result, he could put much of himself into his work, could take an interest in it, because he took complete charge of it. The difficulties he had to overcome, the taste he wanted to express kept his mind alert, and the success of his efforts filled him with joy.

The element of interest and this excitation of intelligence that artisans used to enjoy no longer exist. Mechanization and the division of labor have transformed the worker into a simple operator and have killed the joy of work. The man in a factory yoked to a machine that demands nothing of his brain does his monotonous task sadly, gaining nothing from it but fatigue.

The suppression of intelligent work in the manual trades has had repercussions in the plastic arts. We doubtless owe the abnormal increase in numbers of painters and sculptors, with the general mediocrity which is an inevitable consequence, to a desire to escape mechanization. Two centuries ago many of these people would have been skilled woodworkers, potterymakers, or ironworkers, if these trades had had the same attraction for them as they had for men of those times.

Whatever the significance of these secondary causes of the decline of the manual trades in our day, the principal cause in my opinion is the lack of ideal. The most skilled hand is never more than the servant of thought. Thus, the efforts devoted to making artisans what they were of old will be fruitless, I fear. Even if we succeeded in training adroit workers, well versed in the techniques of their craft, in professional schools, we could do nothing with them if they did not have an ideal within themselves to vivify their labors.

We seem to be far from Cennino Cennini and painting,

and yet we are not. Painting is a craft like carpentry and ironworking, subject to the same rules; those who read attentively the book so well translated by your father will be convinced of this. It will show them, moreover, why he so admired the old masters and also why they have no successors today.

With cordial regards to you, Mottez,
*Renoir*

*Here begins the book on the art, made and composed by Cennino da Colle, in the reverence of God, and of the Virgin Mary, and of St. Eustachius, and of St. Francis, and of St. John the Baptist, and of St. Anthony of Padua, and generally of all the Saints of God, and in the reverence of Giotto, of Taddeo, and of Agnolo the master of Cennino, and for the utility and good and advantage of those who would attain perfection in the arts.*

IN the beginning the omnipotent God created the heaven and the earth, and, above all, animals and food; he created man and woman after his own image, endowing them with all the virtues. But Adam was tempted, and fell through the envy of Lucifer, who, with malice and subtlety, induced him to sin against the commandment of God (first Eve sinned, and then Adam); and God was displeased with Adam, and caused him and his companion to be driven by an angel out of paradise, saying to them, "Because you have disobeyed the commandment which God gave to you, by your labour and exertions shall you support yourselves." Then Adam, knowing the sin he had committed, and being nobly endowed by God as the root and father of us all, discovered, by his wisdom and his necessities, how to live by his own manual exertions. And thus he began by digging, and Eve by spinning. Then followed many necessary arts, different each from the other, and each more scientific than the other; for they could not all be equally so. Now, the most worthy is Science; after which comes an art derived from science, and dependent on the operations of the hand, and this is called Painting, for which we must be endowed with imagination and skill, to discover things (concealed under the shade of nature), and form with the hand, and present to the sight, that which did not before appear to exist. And well does it deserve to be placed in the rank next to science, and to be crowned by Poetry: and for this reason, that the poet, by the help of science, becomes worthy, and free, and able, to compose and bind together or not at pleasure. So to the painter liberty is given to compose a figure, either upright or sitting, or half man half horse, as he pleases, according to his fancy. I have therefore undertaken to adorn this principal science with some jewels, for the benefit of all those persons who feel inclined to learn the various methods, and who worthily and without bashfulness set themselves about it; devoting to the beforementioned science what little God has given me, as an unworthy member and servant of the art of painting.

I Cennino, son of Andrea Cennini, born in the Colle di Valdelsa, was instructed in these arts for twelve years by Agnolo son of Taddeo of Florence, my master, who learned the art from Taddeo his father, the godson of Giotto, whose disciple he had been for twenty-four years. This Giotto introduced the Greek manner of painting among the Latins, and united it to the modern school, and the art became more perfect than it had ever been. In order to assist all those who are desirous of acquiring this art, I shall make notes of all that was taught me by my master Agnolo, and which I have proved with my own hand; invoking first the high omnipotent God,—that is to say, the Father, Son, and Holy Spirit; secondly, that most delightful advocate of all sinners, the Virgin Mary, and St. Luke the Evangelist, the first Christian painter, and my advocate St. Eustachius, and generally all the saints, male and female, of paradise. Amen. (I, 1)

*How some persons study the arts from nobleness of mind, and some for gain*

IT is the stimulus of a noble mind which induces persons to study these arts, made pleasing to them by the love of nature. The intellect delights in invention; and it is nature alone, and the impulse of a great mind, which attracts them, without the guidance of a master. The delight they take in these studies induces them to seek a master, and they gladly dispose themselves to obey him, being in servitude, that they may carry their part to perfection. There are some who follow the arts from poverty and necessity; but those who pursue them from love of the art and true nobleness of mind are to be commended above all others. (I, 2)

*What things are necessary in the pursuit of the arts*

NOW then, you who, possessing noble minds, are lovers of this accomplishment, and who study the arts in general, adorn yourselves first with this vesture,—namely, love, reverence, obedience, and perseverance. And, according to my ability, I shall begin to put you under the direction of a master, to learn as much as in the following pages I can impart to you of what my master taught me. (I, 3)

*Into what parts and members the arts are divided*

I begin with drawing and colouring, which are the foundation of all the arts, and of all the labours of the hand. To these two parts many things are necessary; namely, to know how to grind colours; to use glue; to fasten the cloth on the panel; to prime with chalk; to smooth the surface of the ground of the picture, and to polish it; to make relievos in plaster (*gesso*); to use bole; to gild; to burnish; to temper colours; to lay on flat colours; to powder a drawing; to scrape; to engrave gilding; to rule lines, to colour; to adorn and to varnish pictures. To paint on walls, it is necessary to wet them; to cover them with mortar; to embellish them; to polish them; to design, to colour in fresco and in secco; to temper the colours; adorn and retouch. And I will set forth progressively, according to the little knowledge I have acquired, the rules of the great masters before mentioned relative to these different matters. (I, 4)

*In what manner drawings on panels should be begun*

AS I have before said, you must begin by drawing. It is necessary that you should be accustomed to draw very correctly. In the first place, you must have a panel of box-wood, the size of which should be on every side the length of the hand closed, with the thumb extended, well smoothed and clean,—that is to say, washed with clean water, rubbed and polished with sepia (bone of the cuttle-fish), which the goldsmiths use for marking. When the above-mentioned panel is quite dry, take a sufficient quantity of bones, well pulverised for two hours, and the finer they are ground the better they will be. Then collect the powder, and put it into dry paper; and when you would prime the panel (*ingessare*), take less than half the size of a bean of this bone-dust, mix it up with saliva, and before it is dry spread it with the finger over the surface of the panel. Hold the panel in the left hand; and, with the end of the fore-finger of the right hand, beat upon the panel until you see that it is quite dry, and that the bone-dust is spread all over it equally. (I, 5)

*In what manner you should begin to draw with a stile, and with what light*

THE bones also of the leg and shoulder of mutton are good, burnt as before directed. Then take a stile of silver, or brass with a silver point, sufficiently fine and polished. Then, to acquire command of hand in using the stile, begin to draw with it from a copy as freely as you can, and so lightly that you can scarcely see what you have begun to do, deepening your strokes as you proceed, and going over them repeatedly, to make the shadows. Where you would make it darkest, go over it many times; and, on the contrary, make but few touches on the lights. And you must be guided by the light of the sun, and your eye, and your hand; and without these three things you can do nothing properly. Contrive always when you draw that the light be softened, and the sun strike on your left hand; and in this manner you should draw a short time every day, that you may not become tired or weary. (I, 8)

*How to arrange or accommodate yourself to the light, so as to produce the chiaro-scuro, and give proper relief to your figures*

IF by accident it should happen, that when designing or drawing in chapels, or colouring in other unfavourable places, you cannot have the light on your left hand, or in your usual manner, or give relief to your figures, or design correctly, on account of the arrangement of the windows in these places, from which you are to receive the light,—you must accommodate yourself to the light on which side soever it may be, and give the proper lights and shadows. Or if the light should enter or shine full in your face, make your lights and shades accordingly; or if the light enter at a window larger than the others in the above-mentioned places, adopt always the best light, and, with due consideration, accommodate your painting to it; because, wanting this, your work will be without relief, unskilfully executed, and of little value. (I, 9)

*How drawings with the pen should be practised*

WHEN you have practised drawing in this manner one year, either more or less, according to the pleasure you take in it, you may sometimes draw on paper with a well-made pen. Draw lightly, leaving your lights and your half-lights and your shades gradually, and going over the latter many times with your pen. And if you would have your drawing very beautiful, use a little water-colour, as before directed, with a hair-pencil. Do you know what will be the consequence of this practice of drawing with the pen? It will make you expert, skilful, and capable of making original designs. (I, 13)

*How to draw on tinted paper*

IN order to proceed gradually and begin at the very beginning, and, as it were, the threshold of colouring, you must learn another method of drawing besides those of which we have previously been speaking; and this is called, drawing on tinted paper—either on parchment or paper. The term "tinted" is used because the whole surface of the paper is coloured with the same tint. The tints may be either red, purple, green, azure, grey, flesh-colour, or any colour you please; they all require the same tempering and grinding, and may all be drawn upon in the same manner. It is true that green tints are the most beautiful and most frequently used, both in shading and in the lights. I shall hereafter treat of grinding the colours, of their several natures, and of the medium (*tempera*) they require. I must be brief upon this subject, being desirous of instructing you in drawing and tinting paper. (I, 15)

*Showing how you should endeavour to draw and instruct yourself in design as much as you can*

IT is now requisite that you should copy from models, in order to attain the highest branches of the science. You have made tinted cards. It is necessary for you to adopt this mode. Having practised drawing a sufficient time on tablets, as I have before directed, always study and delight in drawing the best subjects which offer from the works of the great masters. If there are so many good masters in the place where you live, so much the better for you. But I advise you always to select the best and most celebrated; and if you daily imitate his manner, it is scarcely possible but that you will acquire it; for if you copy to-day from this master and to-morrow from that, you will not acquire the manner of either; and as the different style of each master unsettles your mind, your own manner will become fantastic. If you will study this manner to-day and that to-morrow, you must of necessity copy neither perfectly; but if you continually adopt the manner of one master, your intellect must be very dull indeed if you do not find something to nourish it. And it will happen that if nature has bestowed on you any invention, you will acquire a manner of your own, which cannot be other than good, because your hand and your understanding being aways accustomed to gather the flowers, will always avoid the thorns. (I, 27)

*How you should draw continually from nature, as well as from the masters*

REMEMBER that the most perfect guide that you can have and the best direction is to draw from nature: it is the best of all possible examples, and with a bold heart you may always trust to it, especially when you begin to have some knowledge of design. And continuing always and without fail to draw something every day, how little soever it may be, you will certainly attain excellence. (I, 28)

*How you should regulate your manner of living so as to preserve decorum, and keep your hand in proper condition, and what company you should frequent; and how you should select and draw a figure in relief*

YOUR manner of living should be always regulated as if you were studying theology, philosophy, or any other science; that is to say, eating and drinking temperately—at the most twice a day, using light and good food, and but little wine; keeping in good condition, and restraining your hand, preserving it from fatigue, throwing stones or iron bars for instance, and many other things which are injurious to the hand, causing it to shake. There is still another cause, the occurrence of which may render your hand so unsteady that it will oscillate and tremble more than leaves shaken by the wind, and this is, frequenting too much the company of ladies.—Let us return from our digression. Make a pocket of sheets of paper glued together, or of light wood, fit to hold any picture or paper, and this will hold your drawings, and also serve for a desk to draw upon. Then always retire alone, or with companions who are doing as you do, and who will not hinder your work; and the more intellectual these companions are, the better will it be for you. Whether it be in churches or chapels that you begin to draw, consider first what space, or history, or figures, you wish to sketch, and remark where the shades, middle tints, and lights fall; and I must tell you here to shade with ink and water, to leave the ground of the panel for the middle tints, and to use white for the lights. (I, 29)

*In what manner you should begin to draw on paper*

PROCURE some fine charcoal, cut to a point, like a pen or a stile, and the first measure that you take in drawing let it be one of the three parts into which the face is divided, namely, the *with charcoal, and proportion the figure, and fix your drawing with a silver stile*

head, the face, and the chin, with the mouth. And, taking one of these three parts for a guide, proportion the whole figure by it, endeavouring to understand and be governed by these measures; and this is done, because the historical painting, or the figure you copy, may be of large dimensions, and you may be unable to reach with the hand to measure it. You must make use of your understanding, and in this way truth will be your conductor. If you have not proportioned your drawing exactly by the first touches, take a feather, either of a hen or a goose, and, with the feather-part of it, rub and clean away the charcoal from what you have drawn, and the design will be effaced. Begin again from that part the proportions of which appear to agree with the original; and when you see that it is correct, take the silver stile, and retrace the outlines and extremities of your design, and the depths of shade. When you have done this, with the feather-part of the pen remove the charcoal, and your drawing will be fixed by the stile.

(I, 30)

*How to draw and shade on tinted paper in water-colours, and heighten the lights with white*

WHEN you have sufficiently practised shading, take a hair-pencil without a point, and with water and ink, in a small vase, wash over the principal shades, and proceed to deepen them properly. If you find your tint too light, and if your pencil becomes as it were almost dry, yet be not in haste; you will learn to shade by degrees by always returning with your pencil to the darkest parts. Do you know what will happen from this proceeding? If the water have but little colour, and you take pleasure in shading, and do not hurry yourself, your shades will at last appear soft, like smoke. Always remember to keep the pencil flat. When you can shade well, take a drop or two of ink, add it to the water, and stir it well; and then in the same manner fill in the darker shades to their utmost depths—always remembering, while shading, your three divisions, the first consists of the shades, the second of the colour of the ground, and the third of the lights. When you have done this, take a little white lead, well triturated with gum-arabic (hereafter I shall treat of the manner in which this gum should be tempered and dissolved, and I shall also treat of all kinds of vehicles); a very little white will be sufficient. Put some clean water in a little vase; dip your pencil into it, and rub it on the prepared white lead, particularly if it be of good body; then hold the paint by your thumb and finger, and, squeezing the pencil, discharge the colour from it, so that you leave it almost dry. Begin by washing the pencil flat over those places where there ought to be lights and relievos, and go many times over them, but with discretion; then, for the extreme relievos and high lights, take a pointed pencil, and touch them with the point of the pencil dipped in white. Take a small pencil, and with ink clear up the extreme shades and outlines, noses, eyes, hair, and beard. (I, 31)

*The manner of painting on walls, that is, in fresco; and of colouring the faces of young persons*

I will now teach you to colour. I shall begin with painting on walls, and shall teach you step by step the manner in which you ought to proceed. When you are going to paint on walls, which is the most agreeable of all kinds of painting, procure, in the first place, lime and sand, and sift both of them well. If the lime is very rich and fresh, it will require two parts of sand and one of lime. Temper them well together with water, and temper enough to last you fifteen or twenty days. Let the lime rest for some time till it be quite slacked; for if any heat remain in it, it will crack the plaster (*intonaco*). When you are going to lay on the mortar (*ismaltare*), first sweep the wall, and wet it well—you cannot wet it too much; and let the lime be well stirred with a trowel, and spread it over once or twice, till the intonaco becomes quite even on the wall. Afterwards, when you are going to work, remember to make the surface of the mortar very stiff, and rather rough. Then, according to the subject or figures you are going to represent, if the intonaco be dry, take some charcoal and make your design. Adjust the proportions, first striking a line through the middle of the space you intend your picture to occupy. Then strike another (*i.e.,* a horizontal) line, and try whether it be even. And in order to determine whether the line in the centre be straight, you must fix to it a string with a leaden weight at the end. Then put one foot of the large compasses on this string; turn the compasses half round on the under side; then put the point of the compasses on the cross where both lines meet, and make the other half circle above, and you will find that by the lines intersecting each other you will always have a cross on your right hand. There will be a similar cross on your left hand; and a line drawn from the point of intersection of one cross to that of the other will always be a horizontal line. Then draw with charcoal, as I have before directed you, historical pieces and figures, and divide the space on which you are going to paint into squares of equal size. Next take a small and pointed pencil of bristles, with a little ochre, without tempera, as liquid as water, and continue to draw your figures, shading them as you did with water-colours when I taught you to draw, and afterwards brush away the charcoal with a feather.

Then take a little sinopia without tempera, and with a finely pointed pencil mark out the noses, eyes, hair, and all the extremities and outlines of the figures, and let these figures be divided into an equal number of squares; for this will enable you to arrange the figures properly, which you are afterwards to colour. Then make your ornaments and accessories as you please. Take some of the before-mentioned lime, stir it well with a trowel until it be of the consistence of ointment. Then consider how much you can paint in a day; for whatever you cover with the mortar you must finish the same day. It is true that, when you are painting on walls during the damp weather in the spring, the mortar will remain wet until the next day; but if you can help it, do not delay, because when painting in fresco, that which is finished in one day is the firmest and the best, and is the most beautiful work. Then spread over a coat of intonaco rather thin (but not too thin), first wetting the old intonaco. Next take your large hog's hair brush. First steep it in clean water, and wet your mortar with it, and then with a slip of wood as wide as the palm of your hand rub over the intonaco so as to remove the lime where you have put too much, and put more where there is not enough, and thus make your mortar quite smooth. Then wet the mortar with your brush; if necessary, afterwards rub very smoothly and evenly over the intonaco with the point of the trowel. Then place your plumb-line as usual, and measure off an equal space on the intonaco below in the same manner as you did at first. Let us suppose that you can paint in one day the head only of a young male or female saint, such as that of our most holy Lady. Having thus smoothed the wall with your mortar, procure a glazed vessel; the vessels should all be glazed, and shaped like drinking-glasses, with wide feet, that they may stand firmly, and not spill the colours. Take the size of a bean of dark ochre (for there are two kinds of ochre, light and dark) ; and if you have no dark ochre, take light ochre ground very fine, put it into your vase; and take a little black, the size of a lentil, mix it with the ochre; take a little bianco sangiovanni, also the size of a bean, and as much light cinabrese as will lie on the point of a penknife; mix all these colours thoroughly together, and make them very liquid with water, without tempera. Prepare a pencil of hog's bristles, so fine that it may be introduced into the quill of a goose, and with this pencil draw with proper expression the face you are going to paint (remembering that the face is divided into three parts, namely, the forehead, the nose, and the chin, with the mouth) with a little of this colour, which is called at Florence verdaccio, and at Sienna bazzeo; this you should use almost dry. When you have sketched out the form of the face, if the proportions or any other thing should displease you, with a large brush steeped in water rub over the intonaco, and efface and repair what you have done. Then take a little verde terra, very liquid, in another vase, and with a pencil of hog's bristles, without a point, squeezed with the fingers and thumb of the left hand, begin to shade under the chin, and all those parts which should be darkest,—under the lips, the corners of the mouth, under the nose, and under the eyebrow, making the shade darker near the nose, a little on the edge of the eye towards the ear; and in the same manner shading with judgment the whole face and hands, which are hereafter to be coloured with the flesh-colour. Next take a pointed pencil of minever, and perfect all the outlines of the nose, eyes, lips, and ears, with the verdaccio. There are some masters who, when the face is advanced thus far, with a little bianco sangiovanni tempered with water put on the high lights in their proper places; then give the rose-colours (*rossette*) to the lips and cheeks; then wash over the whole with the flesh-colours very liquid with water, and this will complete the colouring of the head. It is a good plan to retouch afterwards the high lights with a little white. Some painters wash over the whole face with the flesh-colour first, on that they put the verdaccio and carnations, and retouch the lights, and the work is finished. This plan is adopted by those only who know but little of the art; but do you pursue the method of colouring which I shall point out to you, because it was adopted by Giotto, the great master, who had Taddeo Gaddi, his godson, for his disciple for twenty-four years; his disciple was Agnolo his son; I was Agnolo's disciple for twelve years, and he shewed me this method, with which Agnolo coloured more agreeably and brilliantly than did Taddeo his father. First take a small vase; put into it equal quantities of bianco sangiovanni and cinabrese, just as much as you think you shall want. Make them very liquid with clean water; then with a soft pencil of bristles, squeezed between the fingers and thumb as before, pass over the face when you have made the touches with verde terra; and with this red colour (*rossetta*) touch in the lips and the colour in the cheeks. My master was accustomed to put the colour in the cheeks nearer the ear than the nose, because it assisted in giving relief to the face, and then he softened it well into the surrounding colours. Then procure three small vases, and make three shades of flesh-colour (*incarnazione*), that is to say, the darkest is to be lighter than the other in regular gradations. Now take some colour from the little vase containing the lightest tint, and with a very soft pencil of bristles without a point, previously squeezed with the fingers, paint in the lights of the face; then take the middle tints of the flesh-colour, and paint the middle tints of the face, hands, and bust, when you paint a naked figure. Afterwards take the third vase of flesh-colour, and go to the edges of the shadows, leaving the verde terra always visible in the extremities, and in this manner softening one tint into the other, until it is all covered as well and as evenly as the nature of the work will permit. But if you would have your work appear very brilliant, be careful to keep each tint of flesh-colour in its place, and do not mix one with another. But seeing others work, and practising with your hand, will make you more expert than any other instructions. When you have painted in these carnations, make a tint much lighter—indeed almost white, and use this above the eyebrow, on the light of the nose, the tip of the chin, and the eyelids; then take a dry pencil of minever, and with pure white put on the lights of the eyes, the point of the nose, and a little on the lips, and so touch tenderly all the lights. Then put a little black into another vase, and with a pencil mark out the outlines of the eyes above the lights of the eyes, and make the holes of the nostrils and the interior of the ear. Then put some dark sinopia into another vase, paint the under outline of the eyes, the contour of the nose, the brows, and the mouth, and shade a little under the upper lip, which must be a little darker than the under. When these outlines are finished, dip the same pencil in verdaccio, and retouch the hair; put on the lights with white, and with light ochre, tempered with water, and a soft brush, cover over the hair as you did the carnations. Mark out the extremities of the shadows with dark ochre, then with a small and very pointed pencil of minever put on the lights of the hair with white and light ochre. Retouch the outlines and extremities of the hair with sinopia as you did on the face, which will finish it. And this is sufficient for you with respect to painting youthful faces. (III, 67)

*Of the proportions of the human figure*

BEFORE I proceed further, I will make you acquainted with the proportions of a man; I omit those of a woman, because there is not one of them perfectly proportioned. First, as I have said before, the face is divided into three parts, namely, the forehead, one; the nose, another; and from the nose to the chin, the third: from the edge of the nose the whole length of the eye, one of these parts; from the corner of the eye to the ear, one part; from one ear to the other, the length of one face; from the chin to the beginning of the throat, one part; the length of the throat, one part; from the fork (*forcella*) of the throat to the top of the shoulder, one face; and the other shoulder the same; from the shoulder to the elbow, one face; from the elbow to the beginning of the hand, one face and one part; the length of the hand, one face; from the fork of the throat to the pit of the stomach, one face; from the pit of the stomach to the navel, one face; from the navel to the beginning of the thigh, one face; from the thigh to the knee, two faces; from the knee to the heel, two faces; from the heel to the sole of the foot, one part; the length of the foot, one face . . . . . . The length of a man is equal to his width with the arms extended. The arm with the hand reaches to the middle of the thigh. The whole length of a man is eight faces and two parts. A man has on his left side one rib less than a woman. Man should be dark, woman fair, &c. . . . . . .

I shall not speak of irrational animals, because they appear to have no certain proportions. Draw them as frequently as you can from nature, and you will ascertain them yourself. And this requires much practice. (III, 70)

*How to colour walls "in secco," and what tempera is proper for that purpose*

ANY of the colours used in painting in fresco may also be used *in secco;* but in fresco some colours cannot be used, as orpiment, cinnabar, azzurro della magna, minio, biacca, verderame, and lacca. Those which may be used in fresco are giallorino, bianco sangiovanni, black, ochre, cinabrese, sinopia, verde terra, and amatisto. Colours used in fresco must be made lighter with bianco sangiovanni. And if you wish the greens to preserve their green tint, make them lighter with giallorino; when you would have them take the colours of sage, add bianco. Those colours which cannot be used in fresco must be made lighter by the addition of biacca, giallorino, or orpiment; but orpiment is very rarely used: indeed I think it superfluous. To make a light blue, take three of the same kind of small vases as I directed you to use when speaking of the carnation tints and cinabrese, and prepare these in the same manner, except that where you then used bianco, you should now use biacca, and temper them all. Two sorts of tempera are good; but one is better than the other. The first tempera consists of the white and yolk of an egg, into which are put some cuttings from the top of a fig-tree; beat them well together; then add some of this tempera moderately, and not in too great quantity, to each of the vases, as if you were diluting wine with water. Then work with your colours, either white, or green, or red, as I directed you in fresco-painting; and proceed with your draperies in the same manner as you did in fresco with tempera, except that you need not wait for it to dry. If you use too much tempera, the colour will be liable to crack, and peel off the wall. Be wise and skilful. Remember before you begin to work, if you wish to make a drapery of lake, or any other colour, take a clean sponge, and having mixed the white and yolk of an egg with about two porringers full of clean water, and beaten them well together; dip the sponge into the tempera and squeeze it half dry, and wash with it the whole of the space on which you mean to paint in secco, and ornament with gold, and then colour it as you please. The second kind of tempera is the yolk of the egg only; and you must know that this tempera is of universal application on walls, on pictures, and in fresco, and you cannot use too much of it, but it would be wise to take a middle course. Before we proceed further, I would have you paint a drapery in secco, in the same manner as you did in fresco, with cinabrese. Now I will give you directions to paint such a one, of ultramarine blue. Take the three vases as usual; into the first put two parts azure and the third biacca; into the third, two parts biacca and one part azure: mix and temper them as I have directed you. Then take an empty vase, that is to say, the second; put into it an equal quantity from each of the others, and stir all well together with a pencil of hog's bristles, or a firm pencil of minever without a point; and with the first colour, that is to say, the darkest, mark out the darkest folds. Take the middle colour, and lay it flat over the middle tints, leaving the lights of the figures. Then take the third colour, and mark out the light folds which come upon the parts in relief, and unite and soften them with each other, as I shewed you how to do in fresco. Take the lightest colour, add to it some biacca, with tempera, and put on the high lights. Then take a little pure biacca, and retouch a few of the highest lights as the shape of the naked figure requires. Afterwards with pure ultramarine glaze the darkest shades and outlines; and in this way paint the drapery, according to its situation and colours, without soiling or mixing them one with another, except to soften them. And in this manner use lake, and all other colours which can be used in secco.

But let us return to our colouring, and from walls proceed to pictures, which are the pleasantest and neatest part of our art. And remember, that he who learns to paint first on walls, and then on pictures, does not become so perfect a master of the art, as when he happens to learn to paint on pictures first, and then on walls. (III, 72)

*In what manner the art of painting pictures should be acquired*

KNOW, that you cannot learn to paint in less time than that which I shall name to you. In the first place, you must study drawing for at least one year; then you must remain with a master at the workshop for the space of six years at least, that you may learn all the parts and members of the art,—to grind colours, to boil down glues, to grind plaster (*gesso*), to acquire the practice of laying grounds on pictures (*ingessare le ancone*), to work in relief (*relevare*), and to scrape (or smooth) the surface (*radire*), and to gild; afterwards to practise colouring, to adorn with mordants, paint cloths of gold, and paint on walls, for six more years,—drawing without intermission on holydays and workdays. And by this means you will acquire great experience. If you do otherwise, you will never attain perfection. There are many who say that you may learn the art without the assistance of a master. Do not believe them; let this book be an example to you, studying it day and night. And if you do not study under some master, you will never be fit for any thing; nor will you be able to shew your face among the masters. (V, 104)

*How to begin to paint pictures*

NOW we are really going to paint pictures. In the first place, a panel of the wood of the poplar, lime, or willow-tree, must be prepared, on which to paint the picture. Let it be made quite smooth: if it be defaced with knots, or if it be greasy, you must cut it away as far as the grease extends, for there is no other remedy. The wood must be very dry; and if it be such a piece that you can boil in a cauldron of clean water, after the boiling it will never split. Let us now return to the knots, or any other defect in the smoothness of the panel. Take some glue (*colla di spicchi*), and about a glassful of clean water, melt and boil two pieces (*spicchi*) in a pipkin free from grease; then put in a porringer some sawdust, and knead it into the glue; fill up the defects or knots with a wooden spatula, and let them remain. Then scrape them with the point of a knife, till they are level with the rest of the panel. Examine if there be any nail, or other thing, that renders the panel uneven, and knock it into the panel; then provide some pieces of tin-plate, like quattrini (small pieces of money), and cover over the iron with them. And this is done that the rust of the iron may not rise through the ground. The surface of the panel cannot be too smooth. Boil some glue, made of parchment-shavings, till the water be reduced to one-third of what it was at first; and when put on the hands, if one hand stick to the other, it is sufficiently boiled. Strain it two or three times. Put half this glue into a pipkin, add a third part water, and boil well together. Then with a hog's-hair pencil, large and soft, pass a coat of the glue over the panel, or foliage, or pyxes (*civori*), or columns, or whatever you work upon, that is to be covered with a ground (*ingessare*), and let it dry. Then take some of your first strong glue (*colla forte*), and pass twice over your work, letting it dry well between each coat of glue, and it will be glued to perfection. Do you know the effect of the first glue? A weak water or liquor is absorbed from it by the wood, which operates exactly as if, when fasting, you eat a few comfits and drank a glass of wine, which gives you an appetite for dinner. So this glue prepares the wood for the glue and grounds to be applied afterwards. (VI, 113)

*How to fasten linen on panels*

HAVING thus spread the glue, get some linen-cloth, old, fine, and white, and free from grease. Take your best glue, cut or tear this linen into large and small strips, soak these in the glue, and spread it with your hands over the surface of the panel; remove the seams, and spread it well with the palms of the hands, and leave it to dry for two days. And remember, it is best to use glue when the weather is dry and windy. Glue is stronger in the winter. For gilding, the weather should be damp and rainy. (VI, 114)

*How you should first draw on the panels with charcoal, and fix your outlines with ink*

HAVING well planed the surface of the ground, and made it as smooth as ivory, the first thing that you should do is, to draw on your panel with those crayons made of charcoal of the willow, which I formerly taught you to make. But you must fasten the charcoal to a stick about the length of your face, which will better enable you to hold it. Have a feather ready, that when any stroke appears to you to be badly drawn, you may efface it with the feather, and draw it again. Draw with a light hand, and shade the hollow parts and the faces as you did with the pencil, and with the same pen with which you made drawings (*penneggiasse*). When you have finished drawing your figures (especially if the picture be of great value, and you expect it to bring you gain and honour), leave it for a day, return many times to examine it, and improve it wherever you find it necessary. When it appears to you correctly drawn (if possible copy from, or look at, any thing like it in pictures painted by good masters, which is no shame to you, if you copy the figures well), gently rub away the charcoal with the feather from the design, so that it may be just seen, and do not rub away too much, lest you should not understand your design. Put a few drops of ink into a glass half full of water, and with a pointed pencil of minever mark over the outline of your design. Then with the feather part of the pen brush away the charcoal. With some more of the ink, and a flat-pointed pencil of minever, shade the depths and the shadows of the face, and you will have made an agreeable design, which will cause all men to fall in love with your works. (VI, 122)

*Conclusion*

*Praying that the most high God, our Lady, St. John, St. Luke the evangelist and painter, St. Eustachius, St. Francis, and St. Anthony of Padua, may give us grace and strength to sustain and bear in peace the cares and labours of this world; and that to those who study this book, they will give grace to study it well and to retain it, so that by the sweat of their brows they may live peaceably, and maintain their families in this world with grace, and finally, in that which is to come, live with glory, for ever and ever. Amen.*

# *The Renaissance*

. . . EACH TIME A GREAT PAINTER DOES A WORK
THAT SEEMS FALSE AND DECEPTIVE, THIS APPARENT FALSENESS
IS YET QUITE CONSONANT WITH TRUTH. AND IF HE PUT MORE TRUTH
INTO IT, THEN IT WOULD BE DECEPTIVE. . . .

*Michelangelo*

# LEON BATTISTA ALBERTI

LEON BATTISTA ALBERTI *was born in Genoa in 1404; he died in 1472. The perfect example of the Renaissance* homo universalis, *he was as much a philosopher as an architect, a mathematician as a humanist. Further, he has left us some comedies and a romance,* Momus, *which deserves to be better known. Famous for his work on architecture,* De re aedificatoria, *he is no less celebrated for his treatises on sculpture and painting. Eminently modern for his day, his work on painting, which we publish at length, constitutes a marked rupture with that of Cennini, who was nonetheless his contemporary. This is the rupture between the Middle Ages and the Renaissance. Alberti abandons all mystical conceptions of painting. With him, the painter puts aside spiritual subjects and turns his eyes to nature. Still, he does not stop aspiring to a supreme beauty, but this beauty has its roots in the terrestrial world. It does not descend from but rather raises the artist to Heaven. Alberti is the first theoretician of the Florentine painting of the* Quattrocento.

## *On Painting*

BECAUSE this [process of] learning may perhaps appear a fatiguing thing to young people, I ought to prove here that painting is not unworthy of consuming all our time and study.

Painting contains a divine force which not only makes absent men present, as friendship is said to do, but moreover makes the dead seem almost alive. Even after many centuries they are recognized with great pleasure and with great admiration for the painter. Plutarch says that Cassander, one of the captains of Alexander, trembled through all his body because he saw a portrait of his King. Agesilaos, the Lacedaemonian, never permitted anyone to paint him or to represent him in sculpture; his own form so displeased him that he avoided being known by those who would come after him. Thus the face of a man who is already dead certainly lives a long life through painting. Some think that painting shaped the gods who were adored by the nations. It certainly was their greatest gift to mortals, for painting is most useful to that piety which joins us to the gods and keeps our souls full of religion. They say that Phidias made in Aulis a god Jove so beautiful that it considerably strengthened the religion then current.

The extent to which painting contributes to the most honourable delights of the soul and to the dignified beauty of things can be clearly seen not only from other things but especially from this: you can conceive of almost nothing so precious which is not made far richer and much more beautiful by association with painting. Ivory, gems and similar expensive things become more precious when worked by the hand of the painter. Gold worked by the art of painting outweighs an equal amount of unworked gold. If figures were made by the hand of Phidias or Praxiteles from lead itself—the lowest of metals—they would be valued more highly than silver. The painter, Zeuxis, began to give away his things because, as he said, they could not be bought. He did not think it possible to come to a just price which would be satisfactory to the painter, for in painting animals he set himself up almost as a god.

Therefore, painting contains within itself this virtue that any master painter who sees his works adored will feel himself considered another god. Who can doubt that painting is the master art or at least not a small ornament of things? The architect, if I am not mistaken, takes from the painter architraves, bases, capitals, columns, façades and other similar things. All the smiths, sculptors, shops and guilds are governed by the rules and art of the painter. It is scarcely possible to find any superior art which is not concerned with painting, so that whatever beauty is found can be said to be born of painting. *But also this, a dignified painting is held in high honour by many so that among all artists some smiths are named, only this is not the rule among smiths.* For this reason, I say among my friends that Narcissus who was changed into a flower, according to the poets, was the inventor of painting. Since painting is already the flower of every art, the story of Narcissus is most to the point. What else can you call painting but a similar embracing with art of what is presented on the surface of the water in the fountain?

Quintilian said that the ancient painters used to circumscribe shadows cast by the sun, and from this our art has grown. There are those who say that a certain Philocles, an Egyptian, and a Cleantes were among the first inventors of this art. The Egyptians affirm that painting was in use among them a good 6000 years before it was carried into Greece. They say that painting was brought to us from Greece after the victory of Marcellus over Sicily. But we are not interested in knowing who was the inventor of the art or the first painter, since we are not telling stories like Pliny. We are, however, building anew an art of painting about which nothing, as I see it, has been written in this age. They say that Euphranor of Isthmus wrote something about measure and about colours, that Antigonos and Xenocrates exchanged something in their letters about painting, and that Apelles wrote to Pelleus about painting. Diogenes Laertius recounts that Demetrius made commentaries on painting. Since all the other arts were recommended in letters by our great men, and since painting was not neglected by our Latin writers, I believe that our ancient Tuscan [ancestors] were already most expert masters in painting.

Trismegistus, an ancient writer, judged that painting and sculpture were born at the same time as religion, *for thus he answered Aesclepius: mankind portrays the gods in his own image from his memories of nature and his own origins.* Who can here deny that in all things public and private, profane and religious, painting has taken all the most honourable parts to itself so that nothing has ever been so esteemed by mortals?

The incredible prices of painted pictures have been recorded. Aristides the Theban sold a single picture for one hundred talents. They say that Rhodes was not burned by King Demetrius for fear that a painting of Protogenes' should perish. It could be said that the city of Rhodes was ransomed from the enemy by a single painting. Pliny collected many other such things in which you can see that good painters have always been greatly honoured by all. The most noble citizens, philosophers and quite a few kings not only enjoyed painted things but also painted with their own hands. Lucius Manilius, Roman citizen, and Fabius, a most noble man, were painters. Turpilius, a Roman knight, painted at Verona. Sitedius, praetor and proconsul, acquired renown as a painter. Pacuvius, tragic poet and nephew of the poet Ennius, painted Hercules in the Roman forum. Socrates, Plato, Metrodorus, Pyrrho were connoisseurs of painting. The emperors Nero, Valentinian, and Alexander Severus were most devoted to painting. It would be too long, however, to recount here how many princes and kings were pleased by painting. Nor does it seem necessary to me to recount all the throng of ancient painters. Their number is seen in the fact that 360 statues, part on horseback and part in chariots, were completed in four hundred days for Demetrius Phalerius, son of Phanostratus. In a land in which there was such a great number of sculptors, can you believe that painters were lacking? I am certain that both these arts are related and nurtured by the same genius, painting with sculpture. But I always give higher rank to the genius of the painter because he works with more difficult things.

However, let us return to our work. Certainly the number of sculptors and painters was great in those times when princes and plebeians, learned and unlearned enjoyed painting, and when painted panels and portraits, considered the choicest booty from the provinces, were set up in the theatres. Finally L. Paulus Aemilius and not a few other Roman citizens taught their sons painting along with the fine arts and the art of living piously and well. This excellent custom was frequently observed among the Greeks who, because they wished their sons to be well educated, taught them painting along with geometry and music. It was also an honour among women to know how to paint. Martia, daughter of Varro, is praised by the writers because she knew how to paint. Painting had such reputation and honour among the Greeks that laws and edicts were passed forbidding slaves to learn painting. It was certainly well that they did this, for the art of painting has always been most worthy of liberal minds and noble souls.

As for me, I certainly consider a great appreciation of painting to be the best indication of a most perfect mind, even though it happens that this art is pleasing to the uneducated as well as to the educated. It occurs rarely in any other art that what delights the experienced also moves the inexperienced. In the same way you will find that many greatly desire to be well versed in painting. Nature herself seems to delight in painting, for in the cut faces of marble she often paints centaurs and faces of bearded and curly headed kings. It is said, moreover, that in a gem from Pyrrhus all nine Muses, each with her symbol, are to be found clearly painted by nature. Add to this that in no other art does it happen that both the experienced and the inexperienced of every age apply themselves so voluntarily to the learning and exercising of it. Allow me to speak of myself here. Whenever I turn to painting for my recreation, which I frequently do when I am tired of more pressing affairs, I apply myself to it with so much pleasure that I am surprised that three or four hours have passed.[1] Thus this art gives pleasure and praise to whoever is skilled in it; riches and perpetual fame to one who is master of it. Since these things are so, since painting is the best and most ancient ornament of things, worthy of free men, pleasing to learned and unlearned, I greatly encourage our studious youth to exert themselves as much as possible in painting.

Therefore, I recommend that he who is devoted to painting should learn this art. The first great care of one who seeks to obtain eminence in painting is to acquire the fame and renown of the ancients. It is useful to remember that avarice is always the enemy of virtue. Rarely can anyone given to acquisition of wealth acquire renown. I have seen many in the first flower of learning suddenly sink to money-making. As a result they acquire neither riches nor praise. However, if they had increased their talent with study, they would have easily soared into great renown. Then they would have acquired much riches and pleasure.

Enough has been said of this up to here. Let us return to our subject. Painting is divided into three parts; these divisions we have taken from nature.

Since painting strives to represent things seen, let us note in what way things are seen. First, in seeing a thing, we say it occupies a place. Here the painter, in describing this space, will say this, his guiding an outline with a line, is circumscription.

Then, looking at it again, we understand that more planes

of the observed body belong together, and here the painter drawing them in their places will say that he is making a composition.

Finally, we determine more clearly the colours and qualities of the planes. Since every difference in them is born from light, we can properly call their representation the reception of light.

Therefore, painting is composed of circumscription, composition and reception of light. In the following we shall treat of them most briefly.

First we will treat of circumscription. Circumscription describes the turning of the outline in the painting. It is said that Parrhasius, the painter who talked with Socrates in Xenophon, was most expert in this and had examined these lines carefully. I say that in this circumscription one ought to take great pains to make these lines so subtly that they can scarcely be seen. The painter Apelles used to practice this and to compete with Protogenes. Because circumscription is nothing but the drawing of the outline, which when done with too apparent a line does not indicate a margin of the plane but a neat cleavage, I should desire that only the movement of the outline be inscribed. To this, I insist, one must devote a great amount of practice. No composition and no reception of light can be praised where there is not also a good circumscription. It is not unusual, however, to see only a good circumscription—that is, a good drawing—which is most pleasant in itself.

Here is a good aid for whoever wishes to make use of it. Nothing can be found, so I think, which is more useful than that veil which among my friends I call an intersection. It is a thin veil, finely woven, dyed whatever colour pleases you and with larger threads in the parallels as you prefer. This veil I place between the eye and the thing seen, so the visual pyramid penetrates through the thinness of the veil. This veil can be of great use to you. Firstly, it always presents to you the same unchanged plane. Where you have placed certain limits, you quickly find the true cuspid of the pyramid. This would certainly be difficult without the intersection. You know how impossible it is to imitate a thing which does not continue to present the same appearance, for it is easier to copy painting than sculpture. You know that as the distance and the position of the centre are changed, the thing you see seems greatly altered. Therefore the veil will be, as I said, very useful to you, since it is always the same thing in the process of seeing. Secondly, you will easily be able to constitute the limits of the outline and of the planes. Here in this parallel you will see the forehead, in that the nose, in another the cheeks, in this lower one the chin and all outstanding features in their place. On panels or on walls, divided into similar parallels, you will be able to put everything in its place. Finally, the veil will greatly aid you in learning how to paint when you see in it round objects and objects in relief. By these things you will be able to test with experience and judgment how very useful our veil can be to you.

Nor will I hear what some may say, that the painter should not use these things, because even though they are great aids in painting well, [they] may perhaps be so made that he will soon be able to do nothing without them.[2] I do not believe that infinite pains should be demanded of the painter, but paintings which appear in good relief and a good likeness of the subject should be expected. This I do not believe can ever be done without the use of the veil. Therefore, let us use this intersection, that is the veil, as we have said. Then, when a painter wishes to try his skill without the veil, he should note first the limits of objects within the parallels of the veil. Or he may study them in another manner by imagining a line intersected by its perpendicular wherever these limits are located. But since the outlines of the planes are frequently unknown to the inexpert painter—doubtful and uncertain as in the faces of man where he does not discern the distance between the forehead and the temples—it would be well to teach him how he can come to understand them.

This is clearly demonstrated by nature. We see in flat planes that each one marks out lights and shades with its lines. Again spherical concave planes are divided into many planes as if chequered with spots of light and shade. Therefore each part with its highlights, divided by those which are dark, would thus appear as many planes. However, if one continuous plane, beginning shadowy, becomes little by little lighter, then note the middle of it with a very fine line so that the method of colouring it will be less in doubt.

Circumscription, which pertains not a little to composition, remains to be treated. For this it is well to know what composition is in painting. I say composition is that rule in painting by which the parts fit together in the painted work. The greatest work of the painter is the *istoria.* Bodies are part of the *istoria,* members are parts of the bodies, planes are parts of the members. Circumscription is nothing more than a certain rule for designing the outline of the planes, since some planes are small as in animals, others are large as those of buildings and colossi.

Concerning the small planes the precepts given up to here will be enough—precepts which we demonstrated when we learned how to use the veil. Perhaps we should find new rules for the larger planes. We must remember what has been said above in the instruction on planes, rays, the pyramid, the intersection, and on the parallels of the pavement, the centric point and line. On the pavement, drawn with its lines and parallels, walls and similar planes which we have called jacent are to be built. Here I will describe most briefly what I do. First I begin with the foundation. I place the width and the length of the wall in its parallels. In this laying out I follow nature. I note that, in any squared body which has right angles, only two conjoined sides can be seen at one time. I observe this in describing the foundations of the walls. I always commence first of all with the nearest plane, the greatest of those which are equidistant from the cross-section. These I put before the others, describing their width and height in those parallels of the pavement in such a way that for as many *braccia* as I choose they occupy as many parallels. To find the middle of each parallel, I find where the diameters mutually intersect. And thus, as I wish, I draw the foundations. Then the height follows by not at all difficult rules. I know the height of the wall contains in itself this proportion, that as much as it is from the place where it starts on the pavement to the centric line, so much it rises upwards. When you wish this quantity of the pavement up to the centric line to be the height of a man, there will, therefore, be these three *braccia.* Since you wish your wall to be twelve *braccia,* you go up three times the distance from the centric line to that place on the pavement. With these rules we shall be able to draw all planes which have angles.

The way in which circles are drawn remains to be treated. Circles are drawn from angles. I do it in this manner. In a space I make a quadrangle with right angles, and I divide the sides of this quadrangle into parts similar to the parts of the base line of the first quadrangle in the painting. From each point to its opposite point I draw lines and thus the space is divided into many small quadrangles. Here I draw a circle as large as I want it so the lines of the small quadrangles and the lines of the circle cut each other mutually. I note all the points of this cutting; these places I mark on the parallels of the pavement in my painting. It would be an extreme and almost never-ending labour to divide the circle in many places with new minor parallels and with a great number of points to complete the circle. For this reason, when I have noted eight or more intersections, I continue the circle in the painting with my mind, guiding the lines from point to point. Would it perhaps be briefer to turn to the shadows? Certainly, if the body which made the shadow were in the middle, located by rule in its place.

We have considered in what way with the aid of the parallels the large angular and round planes are drawn. Since we have finished the circumscription, that is the way of drawing, composition remains to be treated.

It would be well to repeat what composition is. Composition is that rule of painting by which the parts of the things seen fit together in the painting. The greatest work of the painter is not a colossus, but an *istoria. Istoria* gives greater renown to the intellect than any colossus. Bodies are part of the *istoria,* members are parts of the bodies, planes part of the members. The primary parts of painting, therefore, are the planes. That grace in bodies which we call beauty is born from the composition of the planes. A face which has its planes here large and there small, here raised and there depressed—similar to the faces of old women—would be most ugly in appearance. Those faces which have the planes joined in such a way that they take shades and lights agreeably and pleasantly, and have no harshness of the relief angles, these we should certainly say are beautiful and delicate faces.

Therefore, in this composition of planes grace and beauty of things should be intensely sought for. It seems to me that there is no more certain and fitting way for one who wishes to pursue this than to take them from nature, keeping in mind in what way nature, marvellous artificer of things, has composed the planes in beautiful bodies. In imitating these it is well both to take great care and to think deeply about them and to make great use of our above-mentioned veil. When we wish to put into practice what we have learned from nature, we will always first note the limits to which we shall draw our lines.

Up to here we have talked of the composition of planes; members follow. First of all, take care that all the members are suitable. They are suitable when size, function, kind, colour and other similar things correspond to a type of beauty. If in a painting the head should be very large and the breast small, the hand ample and the foot swollen, and the body puffed up, this composition would certainly be ugly to see. Therefore, we ought to have a certain rule for the size of the members. In this measuring it would be useful to isolate each bone of the animal, on this add its muscles, then clothe all of it with its flesh.[3] Here someone will object that I have said above that the painter has only to do with things which are visible. He has a good memory. Before dressing a man we first draw him nude, then we enfold him in draperies. So in painting the nude we place first his bones and muscles which we then cover with flesh so that it is not difficult to understand where each muscle is beneath. Since nature has here carried the measurements to a mean, there is not a little utility in recognizing them. Serious painters will take this task on themselves from nature. They will put as much study and work into remembering what they take from nature as they do in discovering it. A thing to remember: to measure an animate body take one of its members by which the others can be measured. Vitruvius, the architect, measured the height of man by the feet. It seems a more worthy thing to me for the other members to have reference to the head, because I have noticed as common in all men that the foot is as long as from the chin to the crown of the head. Thus one member is taken which corresponds to all the other members in such a way that none of them is non-proportional to the others in length and width.

Then provide that every member can fulfil its function in what it is doing. A runner is expected to throw his hands and feet, but I prefer a philosopher while he is talking to show much more modesty than skill in fencing. *The painter Demon represented hoplites in a content so that you would say one was sweating while another put down his arms and was plainly seen to pant. Ulysses has been painted so that you could recognize his insanity was only feigned and not real.* An *istoria* is praised in Rome in which Meleager, a dead man, weighs down those who carry him. In every one of his members he appears completely dead—everything hangs, hands, fingers and head; everything falls heavily. Anyone who tries to express a dead body—which is certainly most difficult—will be a good painter, if he knows how to make each member of a body flaccid. Thus, in every painting take care that each member performs its function so that none by the slightest articulation remains flaccid. The members of the dead should be dead to the very nails; of live persons every member should be alive in the smallest part. The body is said to live when it has certain voluntary movements. It is said to be dead when the members no longer are able to carry on the functions of life, that is, movement and feeling. Therefore the painter, wishing to express life in things, will make every part in motion—but in motion he will keep loveliness and grace. The most graceful movements and the most lively are those which move upwards into the air.

Again we say that in composition the members ought to have certain things in common. It would be absurd if the hands of Helen or of Iphigenia were old and gnarled, or if Nestor's breast were youthful and his neck smooth; or Ganymede's forehead were wrinkled and his thighs those of an athlete; if Milo, a very strong man, were to have soft and slender flanks; if a figure whose face is fresh and full should have muscular arms and fleshless hands. Anyone painting Achemenides, found by Aeneas on the island, with the face which Virgil describes and the other members not following such consumptiveness, would be a painter to laugh at. For this reason, all the members ought to conform to a certain appropriateness. I should also like the members to correspond to one colour, because it would be little becoming for one who has a rosy, white and pleasant face to have the breast and the other members ugly and dirty. Therefore, in the composition of members we ought to follow what I have said about size, function, kind and colour. Then everything has its dignity. It would not be suitable to dress Venus or Minerva in the rough wool cloak of a soldier; it would be the same to dress Mars or Jove in the clothes of a woman. The antique painters took care in painting Castor and Pollux to make them appear brothers, but in the one a pugnacious nature appeared and in the other agility. They also took pains to show under the robe of Vulcan his handicap of hobbling—so great was their diligence in expressing the function, kind and dignity of whatever they painted.

The fame of the painter and of his art is found in the following—the composition of bodies. Certain things said in the composition of members also apply here. Bodies ought to harmonize together in the *istoria* in both size and function. It would be absurd for one who paints the Centaurs fighting after the banquet to leave a vase of wine still standing in such tumult. [We would call] it a weakness if in the same distance one person should appear larger than another, or if dogs should be equal to horses, or better, as I frequently see, if a man is placed in a building as in a closed casket where there is scarcely room to sit down. For these reasons, all bodies should harmonize in size and in function to what is happening in the *istoria.*

The *istoria* which merits both praise and admiration will be so agreeably and pleasantly attractive that it will capture the eye of whatever learned or unlearned person is looking at it and will move his soul. That which first gives pleasure in the *istoria* comes from copiousness and variety of things. In food and in music novelty and abundance please, as they are different from the old and usual. So the soul is delighted by all copiousness and variety. For this reason copiousness and variety please in painting. I say that *istoria* is most copious in which in their places are mixed old, young, maidens, women, youths, young boys, fowls, small dogs, birds, horses, sheep, buildings, provinces and all similar things. I will praise any copiousness which belongs in that *istoria.* Frequently the copiousness of the painter begets much pleasure when the beholder stands staring at all the things there. However, I prefer this copiousness to be embellished with a certain variety, yet moderate and grave with dignity and truth. I blame those painters who, where they wish to appear copious, leave nothing vacant. It is not composition but dissolute confusion which they disseminate. There the *istoria* does not appear to aim to do something worthy but rather to be in tumult.

Perhaps solitude will be pleasing for one who greatly desires dignity in his *istoria.* The majesty of princes is said to be contained in the paucity of words with which they make their wishes known. Thus in the *istoria* a certain suitable number of bodies gives not a little dignity. Solitude displeases me in *istorie;* nor can I praise any copiousness which is without dignity. *I dislike solitude in* istorie, *nevertheless I value less that copiousness which shrinks from dignity. I strongly approve in an* istoria *that which I see observed by tragic and comic poets. Since they are able, they produce dreams with few characters. However, my judgement will be nothing until the* istoria *[becomes] so filled by the variety of things that nine or ten men are not able to act with dignity. I think pertinent to this the statement of Varro who admitted no more than nine guests to a banquet in order to avoid confusion.*

In every *istoria* variety is always pleasant. A painting in which there are bodies in many dissimilar poses is always especially pleasing. There some stand erect, planted on one foot, and show all the face with the hand high and the fingers joyous. In others the face is turned, the arms folded and the feet joined. And thus to each one is given his own action and flection of members; some are seated, others on one knee, others lying. If it is allowed here, there ought to be some nude and others part nude and part clothed in the painting; but always make use of shame and modesty. The parts of the body ugly to see and in the same way others which give little pleasure should be covered with draperies, with a few fronds or the hand.[4] The ancients painted the portrait of Antigonos only from the part of the face where the eye was not lacking. It is said that Pericles' head was long and ugly, for this reason he —unlike others—was portrayed by painters and sculptors wearing a helmet. Plutarch says that when the ancient painters depicted the kings, if there were some flaw in them which they did not wish to leave unnoticed, they 'corrected' it as much as they could while still keeping a likeness.

Thus I desire, as I have said, that modesty and truth should be used in every *istoria*. For this reason be careful not to repeat the same gesture or pose. The *istoria* will move the soul of the beholder when each man painted there clearly shows the movement of his own soul. It happens in nature that nothing more than herself is found capable of things like herself; we weep with the weeping, laugh with the laughing, and grieve with the grieving. These movements of the soul are made known by movements of the body. Care and thought weigh so heavily that a sad person stands with his forces and feelings as if dulled, holding himself feebly and tiredly on his pallid and poorly sustained members. In the melancholy the forehead is wrinkled, the head drooping, all members fall as if tired and neglected. In the angry, because anger incites the soul, the eyes are swollen with ire and the face and all the members are burned with colour, fury adds so much boldness there. In gay and happy men the movements are free and with certain pleasing inflections. *They praise Euphranor who executed the face and expression of Alexander Paris in which you could easily recognize him as the judge of the goddesses, the lover of Helen and the slayer of Achilles. And even if Demon also attempted to equal him, in his picture you could easily see [Paris to be] angry, unjust, inconstant, and at the same time placable, given to clemency and mercy, proud, humble and ferocious.* They say that Aristides the Theban, equal to Apelles, understood these movements very well. They will certainly be understood by us when we come to know them through study and diligence.

Thus all the movements of the body should be closely observed by the painter. These he may well learn from nature, even though it is difficult to imitate the many movements of the soul. Who would ever believe who has not tried it how difficult it is to attempt to paint a laughing face only to have it elude you so that you make it more weeping than happy? Who could ever without the greatest study express faces in which mouth, chin, eyes, cheeks, forehead and eyebrows all were in harmony with laughter or weeping. For this reason it is best to learn them from nature and always to do these things very rapidly, letting the observer think he sees more than he actually sees.

But let me say something about these movements. Part of this I fabricate out of my own mind, part I have learned from nature. First of all I think that all the bodies ought to move according to what is ordered in the *istoria.* In an *istoria* I like to see someone who admonishes and points out to us what is happening there; or beckons with his hand to see; or menaces with an angry face and with flashing eyes, so that no one should come near; or shows some danger or marvellous thing there; or invites us to weep or to laugh together with them. Thus whatever the painted persons do among themselves or with the beholder, all is pointed toward ornamenting or teaching the *istoria.* Timantes of Cyprus is praised in his panel, the Immolation of Iphigenia, with which he conquered Kolotes. He painted Calchas sad, Ulysses more sad, and in Menelaos, then, he would have exhausted his art in showing him greatly grief stricken. Not having any way in which to show the grief of the father, he threw a drape over his head and let his most bitter grief be imagined, even though it was not seen. They praise the ship painted in Rome by our Tuscan painter Giotto. Eleven disciples [are portrayed], all moved by fear at seeing one of their companions passing over the water. Each one expresses with his face and gesture a clear indication of a disturbed soul in such a way that there are different movements and positions in each one.

Allow me to pass over the movements most briefly. Some movements of the soul are called affections, such as grief, joy and fear, desire and other similar ones. The following are movements of the body. Bodies themselves move in several ways, rising, descending, becoming ill, being cured and moving from place to place. We painters who wish to show the movements of the soul by movements of the body are concerned solely with the movement of change of place. Anything which moves its place can do it in seven ways: up, the first; down, the second; to the right, the third; to the left, the fourth; in depth moving closer and then away; and the seventh going around. I desire all these movements in painting. Some bodies are placed towards us, others away from us, and in one body some parts appear to the observer, some drawn back, others high and others low.

Because there are some who pass all reason in these movements I should like to recount here some things about pose and movement which I have collected from nature. From this we shall clearly understand that they should be used with moderation. Remember how man in all his poses uses the entire body to support the head, heaviest member of all. When he is resting on one foot, this foot always stands perpendicularly under the head like the base of a column, and almost always in one who stands erect the face is turned in the same direction as the feet. I have noted that the movements of the head are almost always such that certain parts of the body have to sustain it as with levers, so great is its weight. Better, a member which corresponds to the weight of the head is stretched out in an opposing part like an arm of a balance. We see that when a weight is held in an extended arm with the feet together like the needle of a balance, all the other parts of the body will displace to counterbalance the weight. I have noticed that in raising the head no one turns his face higher than he would in looking at the zenith; horizontally no one can turn his face past a point where the chin touches the shoulder; the waist is never twisted so much that the point of the shoulder is perpendicular above the navel. The movements of the legs and of the arms are very free in order not to hamper other 'honest' parts of the body. I see in nature that the hands are almost never raised above the head, nor the foot above the knee, nor between one foot and the other is there more space than that of one foot. Remember that when a hand is extended upward that same side of the body even to the feet follows it so that the heel itself is raised off the pavement.

The diligent artist will note many similar things by himself. Perhaps what I have said is so obvious that it may appear superfluous. But, because I have seen not a few err in these things it seemed best not to be silent about them. You will find that in expressing too violent movements and in making the breast and the small of the back visible at the same time in the same figure—a thing which is neither possible nor becoming—some think to be praised because they hear that figures appear most lively which most throw about all their members. For this reason their figures appear hackers and actors without any dignity in the painting. Because of this they are not only without grace and sweetness but moreover they show the too fiery and turbulent imagination of the artist.

The painting ought to have pleasant and graceful movements, suitable to what is happening there. The movements and poses of virgins are airy, full of simplicity with sweetness of quiet rather than strength; even though to Homer, whom Zeuxis followed, robust forms were pleasing even in women. The movements of youth are light, gay, with a certain demonstration of great soul and good force. In men the movements are more adorned with firmness, with beautiful and artful poses. In the old the movements and poses are fatigued; the feet no longer support the body, and they even cling with their hands. Thus each one with dignity has his own movements to express whatever movements of the soul he wishes. For the greatest disturbance of the soul there are similar great movements of the members. This rule of common movements is observed in all animate beings. It would not be fitting to give a plough ox the same movements that you would to Bucephalos, that high-spirited horse of Alexander. Perhaps it would be appropriate in the painting to make Io, who was changed into a cow, run with her tail turned straight back, with her neck erect, and her feet raised.

We have said enough about the movements of animate beings; now, then, since inanimate things move in all those manners which we have stated above, let us treat of them. I am delighted to see some movement in hair, locks of hair, branches, fronds and robes. The seven movements are especially pleasing in hair where part of it turned in spirals as if wishing to knot itself, waves in the air like flames, twines around itself like a serpent, while part rises here, part there. In the same way branches twist themselves now up, now down, now away, now near, the parts contorting themselves like ropes. Folds act in the same way, emerging like the branches from the trunk of a tree. In this they adhere to the seven movements so that no part of the cloth is bare of movement. As I have noted, movements should be moderated and sweet. They should appear graceful to the observer rather than a marvel of study. However, where we should like to find movement in the draperies, cloth is by nature heavy and falls to the earth. For this reason it would be well to place in the picture the face of the wind Zephyrus or Austrus who blows from the clouds making the draperies move in the wind. Thus you will see with what grace the bodies, where they are struck by the wind, show the nude under the draperies in suitable parts. In the other parts the draperies blown by the wind fly gracefully through the air. In this blowing in the wind the painter should take care not to display any drape against the wind. All that I have said about the movements of animate and of inanimate objects I have observed. Once more you have followed with diligence what I have said about the composition of planes, members and bodies.

The reception of light remains to be treated. In the lessons above I have demonstrated at length how light has the power to vary colours. I have taught how the same colour, according to the light and shade it receives, will alter its appearance. I have said that white and black express to the painter shade and light; all other colours for the painter are matter to which he adds more or less shadow or light. Therefore, let us leave the other things. Here we must consider solely how the painter ought to use white and black.

It is said that the antique painters Polygnotos and Timantes used only four colours. Aglaophon was marvelled at because he liked to paint with one simple colour. Few of these great painters would have chosen this small number of colours, for they so valued a large number that they thought a multitude of colors more suitable to a productive artist. I certainly agree that copiousness and variety of colours greatly add to the pleasure and fame of a painting. But I should like the [highest level of attainment] in industry and art to rest, as the learned maintain, on knowing how to use black and white. It is worth all your study and diligence to know how to use these two well, because light and shade make things appear in relief. Thus white and black make painted things appear in relief and win that praise which was given to Nicias the Athenian painter. They say that Zeuxis, a most famous antique painter, was almost the leader of the others in knowing the force of light and shade; little such praise was given to the others. I almost always consider mediocre the painter who does not understand well the strength of every light and shade in each plane. I say the learned and the unlearned praise those faces which, as though carved, appear to issue out of the panel, and they criticize those faces in which is seen no other art than perhaps that of drawing.

I prefer a good drawing with a good composition to be well coloured. Therefore let us study first of all light and shade, and remember how one plane is brighter than another where the rays of light strike, and how, where the force of light is lacking, that same colour becomes dusky. It should also be noted that the shadow will always correspond to the light in another part so that no part of a body is lighted without another part being dark.

As for imitating the bright with white and the shadow with black, I admonish you to take great care to know the distinct planes as each one is covered with light or shadow. This will be well enough understood by you from nature. When you know it well, with great restraint you will commence to place the white where you need it, and, at the same time, oppose it with black. With this balancing of white and black the amount of relief in objects is clearly recognized. Thus with restraint little by little continue raising more white and more black as much as you need.

A good judge for you to know is the mirror. I do not know why painted things have so much grace in the mirror. It is marvellous how every weakness in a painting is so manifestly deformed in a mirror. Therefore things taken from nature are corrected with a mirror. I have here truly recounted things which I have learned from nature.

Remember that on a flat plane the colour remains uniform in every place; in the concave and spherical planes the colour takes variations, because what is here light is there dark, in other places a median colour. This alteration of colours deceives the stupid painters, who, as we have said, think the placing of the lights to be easy when they have well designed the outlines of the planes. They should work in this way. First they should cover the plane out to the outlines as if with the lightest dew with whatever white or black they need. Then above this another and then another and thus little by little they should proceed. Where there is more light, they should use more white; where the light fails the white is lost as if in smoke. In the same way they should do the contrary with black.

But remember, never make any plane so white that it cannot be made whiter. If you should dress a figure in whitest robes, it is best to stop much below the highest whiteness. The painter has nothing other than white with which to show the highest lustre of the most highly polished sword, and only black to show the deepest shadow of night. You will see the force of this by placing white next to black so that vases by this means appear of silver, of gold and of glass and appear to shine in the painting. For this reason I criticize severely all painters who use white and black without much discretion.

It would please me if white were sold to painters at a price higher than the most precious gems. It would certainly be useful if white and black were made from those very large pearls which Cleopatra destroyed in vinegar, so that painters would be, as they ought to be, miserly and good managers and their works would be truthful, sweet and pleasing. I cannot overemphasize the advantage of this frugality to painters. If they should perhaps sin in the distributing of black and white, it is to be held less against one who uses much black than one who does not well spread out white. From day to day follow nature so that horrid and obscure things come to be hated by you; and as in doing you learn, so your hand becomes more delicate in grace and beauty. Certainly by nature we love open and clear things; therefore, close more tightly the way in which it is most easy to sin.

We have treated of white and black. Now we will treat of the other colours, not where all good and tried colours are found like Vitruvius, the architect, but in what way well ground colors are used in painting. They say that Euphranor, an ancient painter, wrote something about colours; it is not found today. Truly, if ever this was written by others, we have dug this art up from under the earth. If it was never written, we have drawn it from heaven. We will continue to use our intellect as we have up to here. I should prefer that all types and every sort of colour should be seen in painting for the great delight and pleasure of the observer. Grace will be found, when one colour is greatly different from the others near it. When you paint Diana leading her troop, the robes of one nymph should be green, of another white, of another rose, of another yellow, and thus different colours to each one, so that the clear colours are always near other different darker colours. This contrast will be beautiful where the colours are clear and bright. There is a certain friendship of colours so that one joined with another gives dignity and grace. Rose near green and sky blue gives both honour and life. White not only near ash and crocus yellow but placed near almost any other gives gladness. Dark colours stand among light with dignity and the light colours turn about among the darks. Thus, as I have said, the painter will dispose his colours.

There are some who use much gold in their *istoria*. They think it gives majesty. I do not praise it. Even though one should paint Virgil's Dido whose quiver was of gold, her golden hair knotted with gold, and her purple robe girdled with pure gold, the reins of the horse and everything of gold, I should not wish gold to be used, for there is more admiration and praise for the painter who imitates the rays of gold with colours. Again we see in a plane panel with a gold ground that some planes shine where they ought to be dark and are dark where they ought to be light. I say, I would not censure the other curved ornaments joined to the painting such as columns, carved bases, capitals and frontispieces even if they were of the most pure and massy gold. Even more, a well perfected *istoria* deserves ornaments of the most precious gems.

Up to here we have treated most briefly of the three parts of painting. We have treated of the circumscription, of the larger and smaller planes, we have treated of colours as we believe them to pertain to the use of the painter. Therefore, we thus express all painting when we say it is made up of these three things: circumscription, composition and the reception of light. (Book II)

# LEONARDO DA VINCI

*LEONARDO DA VINCI (1452–1519) and his work are too well known to be profitably discussed in a few words. The reader will find here the notes that Leonardo drafted on painting, published under the title* Precepts for the Painter *and edited by Edward MacCurdy, the foremost authority on Da Vinci's writings. Paul Valéry said about Leonardo, "The act of the superior artist is to restore, by means of conscious operations, the sensual value and emotive power of things—an act by which the cycle of being which is completely fulfilled is achieved in the creation of forms." It is this "hold" that man takes on nature which characterizes Leonardo's idea on painting. Consequently, art for him is a kind of science, and no longer the celebration of a dogma or an aspiration to a supernatural beauty.*

## *Precepts for the Painter*

PAINTING IS CONCERNED WITH ALL THE TEN ATTRIBUTES OF SIGHT, NAMELY DARKNESS, BRIGHTNESS, SUBSTANCE AND COLOUR, FORM AND PLACE, REMOTENESS AND NEARNESS, MOVEMENT AMD REST; AND IT IS WITH THESE ATTRIBUTES THAT THIS MY SMALL BOOK WILL BE INTERWOVEN.

WHICH is the more difficult: light and shade or good design?

I maintain that a thing which is confined by a boundary is more difficult than one which is free. Shadows have their boundaries at certain stages, and when one is ignorant of this his works will be lacking in that relief which is the importance and the soul of painting. Design is free, in so much as if you see an infinite number of faces they will be all different, one with a long nose and one with a short; the painter therefore must also assume this liberty, and where there is liberty there is no rule. (ms.2038 Bib. Nat. 1r.)

*Painting*

THE mind of the painter should be like a mirror which always takes the colour of the thing that it reflects, and which is filled by as many images as there are things placed before it. Knowing therefore that you cannot be a good master unless you have a universal power or representing by your art all the varieties of the forms which nature produces,—which indeed you will not know how to do unless you see them and retain them in your mind,—look to it, O Painter, that when you go into the fields you give your attention to the various objects, and look carefully in turn first at one thing and then at another, making a bundle of different things selected and chosen from among those of less value. And do not after the manner of some painters who when tired by imaginative work, lay aside their task and take exercise by walking, in order to find relaxation, keeping, however, such weariness of mind as prevents them either seeing or being conscious of different objects; so that often when meeting friends or relatives and being saluted by them, although they may see and hear them they know them no more than if they had met only so much air. (ms.2038 Bib. Nat. 2r.)

The various contrasts of the different degrees of shadows and lights often cause hesitation and confusion to the painter who aspires to imitate and reproduce the things that he sees. The reason is that if you see a white cloth side by side with a black one, it is certain that the part of this white cloth which is next to the black will seem whiter by far than the part that is next to something whiter than itself, and the reason of this is proved in my Perspective.

THE body of the atmosphere is full of an infinite number of the pyramids composed of radiating straight lines which are caused by the boundaries of the surfaces of the bodies in shadow that are found there, and the farther they are away from the object which produces them the more their angle becomes acute. And although they intersect and interlace in their passage, nevertheless they do not become confused with each other but proceed with divergent course, spreading themselves out and becoming diffused through all the surrounding air.

And they are of equal power among themselves, all equal to each, and each equal to all, and by means of them are transmitted the images of the objects, and these are transmitted all in all, and all in each part; and each pyramid receives of itself in each of its smallest parts the whole form of the object which produces it. (ms.2038 Bib. Nat. 6v.)

*Precepts of painting*

LET the sketches for historical subjects be rapid, and the working of the limbs not too much finished. Content yourself with merely giving the positions of these limbs, which you will then be able at your leisure to finish as you please.

(ms.2038 Bib. Nat. 8v.)

Among shadows of equal strength that which is nearest to the eye will seem of less density. (ms.2038 Bib. Nat. 9v.)

ALL colours in distant shadows are indistinguishable and undiscernible.

In the distance all colours are indistinguishable in shadows, because an object which is not touched by the principal light has no power to transmit its image through the more luminous atmosphere to the eye, because the lesser light is conquered by the greater.

For example, we see in a house that all the colours on the surface of the walls are visible instantly and clearly when the windows of the house are open; but, if we go out of the house and look through the windows at a little distance in order to see the paintings on the walls, we shall see instead of them a uniform darkness.

THE painter ought first to exercise his hand by copying drawings by good masters; and having acquired facility in this under the advice of his instructor, he ought to set himself to copy good reliefs, following the rules given below.

*Of drawing from relief*

HE who draws from relief ought to take his position so that the eye of the figure he is drawing is on a level with his own. And this should be done whenever a head has to be drawn from nature, because generally figures or people whom you meet in the streets all have their eyes at the same level as yours, and if you make them higher or lower you will find that your portrait will not resemble them.

*Of the way to draw figures for histories*

THE painter ought always to consider, as regards the wall on which he intends to represent a story, the height of the position where he intends to place his characters, so that when he makes studies from nature for this purpose he should have his eye as much below the thing that he is drawing as the said thing appears in the picture above the eye of the spectator: otherwise the work will be deserving of censure.

*Why a painting can never appear detached as do natural things*

PAINTERS oftentimes despair of their power to imitate nature, on perceiving how their pictures are lacking in the power of relief and vividness which objects possess when seen in a mirror, though as they allege they have colours that for clearness and depth far surpass the quality of the lights and shadows of the object seen in the mirror, arraigning herein not reason but their own ignorance, in that they fail to recognise the impossibility of a painted object appearing in such relief as to be comparable to the objects in the mirror, although both are on a flat surface unless they are seen by a single eye.

(ms.2038 Bib. Nat. 10r.)

EVERY bodily form as far as concerns the function of the eye is divided into three parts, namely substance, shape and colour. The image of its substance projects itself farther from its source than its colour or its shape; the colour also projects itself farther than the shape, but this law does not apply to luminous bodies.

The above proposition is clearly shown and confirmed by experience, for if you see a man near at hand you will be able to recognise the character of the substance of the shape and even of the colour, but, if he goes some distance away from you, you will no longer be able to recognise who he is because his shape will lack character, and if he goes still farther away you will not be able to distinguish his colour but he will merely seem a dark body, and farther away still he will seem a very small round dark body. He will appear round because distance diminishes the various parts so much as to leave nothing visible except the greater mass. The reason of this is as follows:—We know very well that all the images of objects penetrate to the imprensiva through a small aperture in the eye; therefore if the whole horizon *a d* enters through a similar aperture and the object *b c* is a very small part of this horizon, what part must it occupy in the minute representation of so great a hemisphere? And since luminous bodies have more power in darkness than any others it is

THE QUESTION OF THE ORIGIN OF PAINTING IS
A DIFFICULT ONE. . . . THE EGYPTIANS CLAIM THEY INVENTED IT
SIX THOUSAND YEARS BEFORE IT CAME INTO GREECE;
BUT THIS IS A VAIN PRETENSION.

*Pliny the Elder*

WE HAVE OLD PAINTINGS WHOSE COLORS ARE WORKED WITH UTTER
SIMPLICITY AND WHICH HAVE NO VARIETY IN THEIR TONES, BUT
THE LINES ARE DRAWN TO PERFECTION, GIVING THESE WORKS GREAT CHARM.

*Dionysius of Halicarnassus*

PAINTING IS AN IMAGE THAT PRESENTS THE APPEARANCE OF AN OBJECT—TO PAINT IS TO FEIGN.

*Isidorus*

IT'S A SAD THING TO PAINT ONLY IN WORDS.

*Lucian*

O YOU WHO ARE SPLENDID AS THE SUN, MOST BELOVED AND ALL-GRACIOUS MOTHER OF GOD, MARY!

*Dionysius of Phourna-Agrapha*

IN EXECUTING HUMAN FIGURES, . . . MEN TRY TO ASSURE ETERNAL REMEMBRANCE FOR THE VIRTUES OF THOSE THEY HONOR.

*Eusebius*

YOUR PAINTINGS SHOULD BE ORNAMENTED
WITHOUT SACRIFICING THE NATURAL.

*Theophilus*

. . . WHAT GOD INTENDED TO CREATE FOR THE PRAISE AND GLORY OF HIS NAME, A PEOPLE DEVOTED TO GOD HAS RESTORED TO HIS WORSHIP.

*Theophilus*

In die scõ pasce
ad missam. offiñ.
Esurrexi
et adhuc tecum
sum alleluia posuisti sup
me manum tu am allelu
ia mirabilis facta est

REMEMBER THAT THE MOST PERFECT GUIDE THAT YOU CAN HAVE AND THE BEST DIRECTION IS TO DRAW FROM NATURE.

*Cennini*

IC
XC

. . . PAINTING IS MOST USEFUL TO THAT PIETY WHICH
JOINS US TO THE GODS AND KEEPS OUR SOULS FULL OF RELIGION.

*Alberti*

PERSPECTIVE IS THE BRIDLE AND RUDDER OF ART.

*Leonardo*

FOR THE GREATEST GRACE AND LIFE THAT
A PICTURE CAN HAVE, IT MUST EXPRESS MOTION:
WHICH THE PAINTERS CALL THE SPIRIT OF A PICTURE.

*Lomazzo*

DESIGN, OR AS IT IS CALLED BY ANOTHER NAME, DRAWING,
CONSTITUTES THE FOUNTAIN-HEAD AND SUBSTANCE OF PAINTING . . .

*Michelangelo*

FOR ART STANDETH FIRMLY FIXED IN NATURE, AND
WHOSO CAN REND HER FORTH THENCE, HE ONLY POSSESSETH HER.

*Dürer*

THE EYE MUST ALWAYS BE ATTENTIVE TO TINTS . . .

*Dolce*

necessary, since the aperture of the sight is considerably in shadow, as is the nature of all holes, that the images of distant objects intermingle within the great light of the sky, or if it should be that they remain visible they appear dark and black, as every small body must when seen in the limpidity of the air. (ms.2038 Bib. Nat. 12v.)

[*Images in the air*]

ALL bodies together and each of itself fill the surrounding air with an infinite number of their images which are all in all this air, and all in the parts of it, bearing with them the nature of the body, the colour and the form of their cause.

Perspective is the bridle and rudder of painting.

(ms.2038 Bib. Nat. 13r.)

SHADOWS which you see with difficulty, and whose boundaries you cannot define—but which you only apprehend and reproduce in your work with some hesitation of judgment—these you should not represent as finished or sharply defined, for the result would be that your work would seem wooden.

*Of reflection*

REFLECTIONS are caused by bodies of a bright nature and of a smooth and half-opaque surface, which when struck by the light drive it back again to the first object like the rebound of a ball.

*Of where there cannot be luminous reflection*

ALL solid bodies have their surfaces covered by various degrees of light and shadow. The lights are of two kinds: the one is called original the other derived. Original I call that which proceeds from the flame of the fire, or from the light of the sun, or of the atmosphere. Derived light is the light reflected. But, to return to the promised definition, I say that there is no luminous reflection on the side of the body which is turned toward objects in shadow such as shaded scenes, meadows with grasses of varying height, green or bare woods —for these, although the part of each branch turned to the original light is imbued with the attributes of this light, have nevertheless so many shadows cast by each branch separately, and so many shadows cast by one branch on another, that in the whole mass there results such a depth of shadow that the light is as nothing; hence objects such as these cannot throw any reflected light upon bodies opposite to them.

(ms.2038 Bib. Nat. 14v.)

THE youth ought first to learn perspective, then the proportions of everything, then he should learn from the hand of a good master in order to accustom himself to good limbs; then from nature in order to confirm for himself the reasons for what he has learnt; then for a time he should study the works of different masters; then make it a habit to practise and work at his art.

How the first picture was nothing but a line which surrounded the shadow of a man made by the sun upon a wall.

How historical pictures ought not to be crowded and confused by many figures.

How old men should be shown with slow listless movements, with the legs bent at the knees when they are standing up, with the feet parallel and separated one from another, the spine bent low, the head leaning forward, and the arms not too far apart.

How women should be represented in modest attitudes, with legs close together, arms folded, and with their heads low and bending sideways.

How old women should be represented as bold, with swift passionate movements like the infernal furies, and these movements should seem quicker in the arms and heads than in the legs.

Little children should be represented when sitting as twisting themselves about with quick movements, and in shy, timid attitudes when standing up.

HOW one ought not to give drapery a confusion of many folds, but only make them where it is held by the hands or arms, and the rest may be suffered to fall simply where its nature draws it: and do not let the contour of the figure be broken by too many lines or interrupted folds.

How draperies should be drawn from nature: that is, if you wish to represent woollen cloth draw the folds from the same material, and if it is to be silk, or fine cloth, or homespun, or of linen or crape, show the different nature of the folds in each; and do not make a costume as many make it upon models covered with pieces of paper or thin leather, for you will be deceiving yourself greatly.

(ms.2038 Bib. Nat. 17v.)

*Of the three kinds of perspective*

PERSPECTIVES are of three kinds. The first has to do with the causes of the diminution or as it is called the diminishing perspective of objects as they recede from the eye. The second the manner in which colours are changed as they recede from the eye. The third and last consists in defining in what way objects ought to be less carefully finished as they are farther away. And the names are these:

Linear Perspective
Perspective of Colour
Vanishing Perspective.

*Of the way to present distant objects in painting*

IT is evident that the part of the atmosphere which lies nearest the level ground is denser than the rest, and that the higher it rises the lighter and more transparent it becomes.

In the case of large and lofty objects which are some distance away from you, their lower parts will not be much seen, because the line by which you should see them passes through the thickest and densest portion of the atmosphere. But the summits of these heights are seen along a line which, although when starting from your eye it is projected through the denser atmosphere, yet since it ends at the highest summit of the object seen, concludes its course in an atmosphere far more rarefied than that of its base. And consequently the farther away from you this line extends from point to point the greater is the change in the finer quality of the atmosphere.

Do you, therefore, O painter, when you represent mountains, see that from hill to hill the bases are always paler than the summits, and the farther away you make them one from another let the bases be paler in proportion, and the loftier they are the more they should reveal their true shape and colour. (ms.2038 Bib. Nat. 18r.)

HOW the atmosphere should be represented as paler in proportion as you see it extending lower:

Since the atmosphere is dense near the ground, and the higher it is the finer it becomes, therefore when the sun is in the east and you look towards the west, taking in a part to the north and to the south, you will see that this dense air receives more light from the sun than the finer air, because the rays encounter more resistance. And if your view of the horizon is bounded by a low plain, that farthest region of the sky will be seen through that thicker whiter atmosphere, and this will destroy the truth of the colour as seen through such a medium; and the sky will seem whiter there than it does overhead, where the line of vision traverses a lesser space of atmosphere charged with thick vapours. But if you look towards the east the atmosphere will appear darker in proportion as it is lower, for in this lower atmosphere the luminous rays pass less freely.

How shadows are distributed in different positions, and of the objects situated in them:

If the sun is in the east and you look towards the west you will see that all the things which are illuminated are entirely deprived of shadow, because what you are looking at is what the sun sees.

And if you look to the south and the north you will see that all the bodies are surrounded by light and shade, because you are looking both at the part that does not see and the part that sees the sun. And if you look towards the pathway of the sun all the objects will present their shaded side to you because this side cannot be seen by the sun.

*Of the way to represent a night scene*

WHATEVER is entirely deprived of light is all darkness. When such is the condition of night, if you wish to represent a scene therein, you must arrange to introduce a great fire there, and then the things which are nearest to the fire will be more deeply tinged with its colour, for whatever is nearest to the object partakes most fully of its nature; and making the fire of a reddish colour you should represent all the things illuminated by it as being also of a ruddy hue, while those which are farther away from the fire should be dyed more deeply with the black colour of the night. The figures which are between you and the fire will appear dark against the brightness of the flame, for that part of the object which you perceive is coloured by the darkness of the night, and not by the brightness of the fire; those which are at the sides should be half in shadow and half in ruddy light; and those visible beyond the edge of the flames will all be lit up with ruddy light against a dark background. As for their actions, show those who are near it making a screen with hands and cloaks as a protection against the unbearable heat, with faces turned away as though on the point of flight; while of those farther away you should show a great number pressing their hands upon their eyes, hurt by the intolerable glare. (ms.2038 Bib. Nat. 18v.)

WHY of two objects of equal size the painted one will look larger than that in relief:

This proposition is not so easy to expound as many others, but I will nevertheless attempt to prove it, if not completely then in part. Diminishing perspective demonstrates by reason that objects diminish in proportion as they are farther away from the eye, and this theory is entirely confirmed by experience. Now the lines of sight which are between the object and the eye are all intersected at a uniform boundary when they reach the surface of the painting; while the lines which pass from the eye to the piece of sculpture have different boundaries and are of varying lengths. The line which is the longest extends to a limb which is farther away than the rest, and consequently this limb appears smaller; and there are many lines longer than others, for the reason that there are many small parts one farther away than another, and being farther away these of necessity appear smaller, and by appearing smaller they effect a corresponding decrease in the whole mass of the object. But this does not happen in the painting, because as the lines of sight end at the same distance it follows that they do not undergo diminution, and as the parts are not themselves diminished they do not lessen the whole mass of the object, and consequently the diminution is not perceptible in the painting as it is in sculpture.

(ms.2038 Bib. Nat. 19r.)

*How white bodies ought to be represented*

WHEN you are representing a white body surrounded by ample space, since the white has no colour in itself it is tinged and in part transformed by the colour of what is set over against it. If you are looking at a woman dressed in white in the midst of a landscape the side of her that is exposed to the sun will be so dazzling in colour that parts of it, like the sun itself, will cause pain to the sight, and as for the side exposed to the atmosphere—which is luminous because of the rays of the sun being interwoven with it and penetrating it—since this atmosphere is itself blue, the side of the woman which is exposed to it will appear steeped in blue. If the surface of the ground near to her be meadows, and the woman be placed between a meadow lit by the sun and the sun itself, you will find that all the parts of the folds [of her dress] which are turned towards the meadow will be dyed by the reflected rays to the colour of the meadow; and thus she becomes changed into the colours of the objects near, both those luminous and those non-luminous.

*How to represent the limbs*

MAKE muscular such limbs as have to endure fatigue, and those which are not so used make without muscles and soft.

*Of the action of figures*

MAKE figures with such action as may be sufficient to show what the figure has in mind; otherwise your art will not be worthy of praise. (ms.2038 Bib. Nat. 20r.)

*Of the choice of the light which gives a grace to faces*

IF you have a courtyard which, when you so please, you can cover over with a linen awning, the light will then be excellent. Or when you wish to paint a portrait, paint it in bad weather, at the fall of the evening, placing the sitter with his back to one of the walls of the courtyard. Notice in the streets at the fall of the evening when it is bad weather the faces of the men and women—what grace and softness they display! Therefore, O painter, you should have a courtyard fitted up with the walls tinted in black and with the roof projecting forward a little beyond the wall; and the width of it should be ten braccia, and the length twenty braccia, and the height ten braccia; and you should cover it over with the awning when the sun is on it, or else you should make your portrait at the hour of the fall of the evening when it is cloudy or misty, for the light then is perfect.

*Why faces at a distance appear dark*

WE see clearly that all the images of the visible things both large and small which serve us as objects enter to the sense through the tiny pupil of the eye. If, then, through so small an entrance there passes the image of the immensity of the sky and of the earth, the face of man—being almost nothing amid such vast images of things, because of the distance which diminishes it—occupies so little of the pupil as to remain indistinguishable; and having to pass from the outer surface to the seat of the sense through a dark medium, that is, through the hollow cells which appear dark, this image when not of a strong colour is affected by the darkness through which it passes, and on reaching the seat of the sense it appears dark.

No other reason can be advanced to account for the blackness of this point in the pupil; and since it is filled with a moisture transparent like the air, it acts like a hole made in a board; and when looked into it appears black, and the objects seen in the air, whether light or dark, become indistinct in the darkness.

*Of the surrounding of bodies with various shades of shadow*

TAKE care that the shadows cast upon the surfaces of bodies by different objects are always undulating with varying curves produced by the variety of the limbs that create the shadows and of the object that receives the shadow.

*Of the essential nature of shadow*

SHADOW partakes of the nature of universal things which are all more powerful at their beginning and grow weaker towards the end. I refer to the beginnings of all forms and qualities visible or invisible, and not of things brought from small beginnings to a mighty growth by time, as a great oak would be which has its feeble beginning in a tiny acorn; though I would rather say the oak is most powerful at the spot where it is born in the ground, for there is the place of its greatest growth. Darkness, therefore, is the first stage of shadow and light is the last. See, therefore, O painter, that you make your shadow darkest near to its cause and make the end of it become changed into light so that it seems to have no end.

How the shadows cast by particular lights should be avoided because their ends are like their beginnings:

The shadows cast by the sun or other particular lights do not impart grace to the body to which they belong, but rather leave the parts separated in a state of confusion with a visible boundary of shadow and light. And the shadows have the same strength at the end that they had at the beginning.

(ms.2038 Bib. Nat. 21v.)

*What shadow and light are*

SHADOW is the absence of light; it is simply the obstruction caused by opaque bodies opposed to luminous rays. Shadow is of the nature of darkness, light is of the nature of brightness. The one hides and the other reveals. They are always in company attached to the bodies. And shadow is more powerful than light for it impedes and altogether deprives objects of brightness, whereas brightness can never altogether drive away shadow from bodies, that is from opaque bodies.

WHAT difference there is between a shadow inseparable from a body and a cast shadow:

An inseparable shadow is one which is never parted from the illuminated bodies, as is the case with a ball, for when it is in the light it always has one of its sides covered by shadow and this shadow never separates from it through any change in the position of the ball. A cast shadow may or may not be produced by the body itself. Let us suppose the ball to be at a distance of a braccio from the wall and the light to be coming from the opposite side: this light will throw just as broad a shadow upon the wall as upon the side of the ball that faces the wall. Part of a cast shadow will not be visible when the light is below the ball, for its shadow will then pass towards the sky and finding there no obstruction in its course will become lost. (ms.2038 Bib. Nat. 22r.)

*Of the ten attributes of sight which all find expression in painting*

PAINTING is concerned with all the ten attributes of sight, namely darkness and brightness, substance and colour, form and place, remoteness and nearness, movement and rest; and it is with these attributes that this my small book will be interwoven, recalling to the painter by what rules and in what way he ought by his art to imitate all things that are the work of nature and the adornment of the world.

*How the painter ought to practise himself in the perspective of colours*

AS a means of practising this perspective of the variation and loss or diminution of the proper essence of colours, take, at distances a hundred braccia apart, objects standing in the landscape, such as trees, houses, men and places, and in front of the first tree fix a piece of glass so that it is quite steady, and then let your eye rest upon it and trace out a tree upon the glass above the outline of the tree; and afterwards remove the glass so far to one side that the actual tree seems almost to touch the one that you have drawn. Then colour your drawing in such a way that the two are alike in colour and form, and that if you close one eye both seem painted on the glass and the same distance away. Then proceed in the same way with a second and a third tree at distances of a hundred braccia from each other. And these will always serve as your standards and teachers when you are at work on pictures where they can be applied, and they will cause the work to be successful in its distance.

But I find it is a rule that the second is reduced to four-fifths the size of the first when it is twenty braccia distant from it.

*Of undulating movements and equipoise in human figures and figures of animals*

WHENEVER you make a figure of a man or of some graceful animal remember to avoid making it seem wooden; that is it should move with counterpoise and balance in such a way as not to seem a block of wood.

Those whom you wish to represent as strong should not be shown thus except in their manner of turning their heads upon their shoulders. (ms.2038 Bib. Nat. 22v.)

*Of linear perspective*

LINEAR perspective has to do with the function of the lines of sight, proving by measurement how much smaller is the second object than the first and the third than the second, and so on continually until the limit of things seen. I find by experience that if the second object is as far distant from the first as the first is from your eye, although as between themselves they may be of equal size, the second will seem half as small again as the first; and if the third object is equal in size to the second, and it is as far beyond the second as the second is from the first, it will appear half the size of the second; and thus by successive degrees at equal distances the objects will be continually lessened by half, the second being half the first—provided that the intervening space does not amount to as much as twenty braccia; for at the distance of twenty braccia a figure resembling yours will lose four-fifths of its size, and at a distance of forty braccia it will lose nine-tenths, and nineteen-twentieths at sixty braccia, and so by degrees it will continue to diminish, when the plane of the picture is twice your own height away from you, for if the distance only equals your own height there is a great difference between the first set of braccia and the second.

*Why an object when placed close to the eye will have its edges indistinct*

ALL those objects opposite to the eye which are too near to it will have their edges difficult to discern, as happens when objects are near to the light and cast a large and indistinct shadow, even so this does when it has to judge of objects outside it: in all cases of linear perspective its action is similar to that of light. The reason of this is that the eye has one principal line [of vision] which dilates as it acquires distance, and embraces with exactness of perception large things far away as it does small things close at hand. The eye however sends out a multitude of lines on either side of this principal centre-line, and these have less power to discern correctly as they are farther from the centre in this radiation. It follows therefore when an object is placed close to the eye that at that stage of nearness to the principal line of vision this is not capable of distinguishing the edges of the object, and so these edges must needs find themselves amid the lines that have but a poor power of comprehension. Their part in the functions of the eye is like that of setters at the chase, who start the prey but cannot catch it. So while they cannot themselves apprehend them they are a reason why the principal line of vision is diverted to the objects touched by these lines.

It follows therefore that the objects which have their edges judged by these lines are indistinct.

(ms.2038 Bib. Nat. 23v.)

*Of the way to represent a scene correctly*

TAKE a piece of glass of the size of a half sheet of royal folio paper, and fix it well in front of your eyes, that is between your eye and the object that you wish to portray. Then move away until your eye is two-thirds of a braccio away from the piece of glass, and fasten your head by means of an instrument in such a way as to prevent any movement of it whatsoever. Then close or cover up one eye, and with a brush or a piece of red chalk finely ground mark out on the glass what is visible beyond it; afterwards copy it by tracing on paper from the glass, then prick it out upon paper of a better quality and paint it if you so desire, paying careful attention to the aerial perspective.

*A way of learning how to place a figure well*

IF you wish thoroughly to accustom yourself to correct and good positions for your figures, fasten a frame or loom divided into squares by threads between your eye and the nude figure which you are representing, and then make the same squares upon the paper where you wish to draw the said nude but very faintly. You should then place a pellet of wax on a part of the network to serve as a mark which as you look at your model should always cover the pit of the throat, or if he should have turned his back make it cover one of the vertebrae of the neck. And these threads will instruct you as to all the parts of the body which in each attitude are found below the pit of the throat, below the angles of the shoulders, below the breasts, the hips and the other parts of the body; and the transverse lines of the network will show you how much higher the figure is above the leg on which it is posed than above the other, and the same with the hips, the knees and the feet. But always fix the net by a perpendicular line and then see that all the divisions that you see the nude take in the network, the nude that you draw takes in the network of your sketch. The squares you draw may be as much smaller than those of the network in proportion as you wish your figure to be less than life size: then keep in mind in the figures that you make, the rule of the corresponding proportions of the limbs as the network has revealed it to you, and this should be three and a half braccia in height and three wide, at a distance of seven braccia from you and one from the nude figure.

(ms.2038 Bib. Nat. 24r.)

*How the mirror is the master of painters*

WHEN you wish to see whether the general effect of your picture corresponds with that of the object represented after nature, take a mirror and set it so that it reflects the actual thing, and then compare the reflection with your picture, and consider carefully whether the subject of the two images is in conformity with both, studying especially the mirror. The mirror ought to be taken as a guide—that is, the flat mirror—for within its surface substances have many points of resemblance to a picture; namely, that you see the picture made upon one plane showing things which appear in relief, and the mirror upon one plane does the same. The picture is one single surface, and the mirror is the same.

The picture is intangible, inasmuch as what appears round and detached cannot be enclosed within the hands, and the mirror is the same. The mirror and the picture present the images of things surrounded by shadow and light, and each alike seems to project considerably from the plane of its surface. And since you know that the mirror presents detached things to you by means of outlines and shadows and lights, and since you have moreover amongst your colours more powerful shadows and lights than those of the mirror, it is certain that if you but know well how to compose your picture it will also seem a natural thing seen in a great mirror. (ms.2038 Bib. Nat. 24v.)

OF the poor excuse made by those who falsely and unworthily get themselves styled painters:

There is a certain class of painters who though they have given but little attention to study claim to live in all the beauty of gold and azure. These aver—such is their folly!—that they are not able to work up to their best standard because of the poor payment, but that they have the knowledge and could do as well as any other if they were well paid.

But see now the foolish folk! They have not the sense to keep by them some specimen of their good work so that they may say, 'this is at a high price, and that is at a moderate price and that is quite cheap', and so show that they have work at all prices. (ms.2038 Bib. Nat. 25r.)

*Of aerial perspective*

THERE is another kind of perspective which I call aerial, because by the difference in the atmosphere one is able to distinguish the various distances of different buildings when their bases appear to end on a single line, for this would be the appearance presented by a group of buildings on the far side of a wall, all of which as seen above the top of the wall look to be the same size; and if in painting you wish to make one seem farther away than another you must make the atmosphere somewhat heavy. You know that in an atmosphere of uniform density the most distant things seen through it, such as the mountains, in consequence of the great quantity of atmosphere which is between your eye and them, will appear blue, almost of the same colour as the atmosphere when the sun is in the east. Therefore you should make the building which is nearest above the wall of its natural colour, and that which is more distant make less defined and bluer; and one which you wish should seem as far away again make of double the depth of blue, and one you desire should seem five times as far away make five times as blue. And as a consequence of this rule it will come about that the buildings which above a given line appear to be of the same size will be plainly distinguished as to which are the more distant and which larger than the others.

*How the painter is not worthy of praise unless he is universal*

WE may frankly admit that certain people deceive themselves who apply the title 'a good master' to a painter who can only do the head or the figure well. Surely it is no great achievement if by studying one thing only during his whole lifetime he attain to some degree of excellence therein! But since, as we know, painting embraces and contains within itself all the things which nature produces or which result from the fortuitous actions of men, and in short whatever can be comprehended by the eyes, it would seem to me that he is but a poor master who makes only a single figure well.

For do you not see how many and how varied are the actions which are performed by men alone? Do you not see how many different kinds of animals there are, and also of trees and plants and flowers? What variety of hilly and level places, of springs, rivers, cities, public and private buildings; of instruments fitted for man's use; of divers costumes, ornaments and arts?—Things which should be rendered with equal facility and grace by whoever you wish to call a good painter.

*Of drawing*

WHICH is better—to draw from nature or from the antique?

And which is more difficult—the lines or the light and shade? (ms.2038 Bib. Nat. 25v.)

*Of studying as soon as you are awake or before you go to sleep in bed in the dark*

I have proved in my own case that it is of no small benefit on finding oneself in bed in the dark to go over again in the imagination the main outlines of the forms previously studied, or of other noteworthy things conceived by ingenious speculation; and this exercise is entirely to be commended, and it is useful in fixing things in the memory.

HOW the painter ought to be desirous of hearing every man's opinion as to the progress of his work:

Surely when a man is painting a picture he ought not to refuse to hear any man's opinion, for we know very well that though a man may not be a painter he may have a true conception of the form of another man, and can judge aright whether he is hump-backed or has one shoulder high or low, or whether he has a large mouth or nose or other defects.

Since then we recognise that men are able to form a true judgment as to the works of nature, how much the more does it behove us to admit that they are able to judge our faults.

For you know how much a man is deceived in his own works, and if you do not recognise this in your own case observe it in others and then you will profit by their mistakes. Therefore you should be desirous of hearing patiently the opinions of others, and consider and reflect carefully whether or no he who censures you has reason for his censure; and correct your work if you find that he is right, but if not, then let it seem that you have not understood him, or, in case he is a man whom you esteem, show him by argument why it is that he is mistaken.

HOW in works of importance a man should not trust so entirely to his memory as to disdain to draw from nature:

Any master who let it be understood that he could himself recall all the forms and effects of nature would certainly appear to me to be endowed with great ignorance, considering that these effects are infinite and that our memory is not of so great capacity as to suffice thereto.

Do you therefore, O painter, take care lest the greed for gain prove a stronger incentive than renown in art, for to gain this renown is a far greater thing than is the renown of riches.

For these, then, and other reasons which might be given, you should apply yourself first of all to drawing in order to present to the eye in visible form the purpose and invention created originally in your imagination; then proceed to take from it or add to it until you satisfy yourself; then have men arranged as models draped or nude in the way in which you have disposed them in your work; and make the proportions and size in accordance with perspective, so that no part of the work remains that is not so counselled by reason and by the effects in nature.

And this will be the way to make yourself renowned in your art.

AN object which is represented in white and black will appear in more pronounced relief than any other: and therefore I would remind you, O painter, that you should clothe your figures in as bright colours as you can, for if you make them dark in colour they will be only in slight relief and be very little visible at a distance. This is because the shadows of all objects are dark, and if you make a garment dark there will be only a slight difference between its lights and shades, whereas with the bright colours there are many grades of difference. (ms.2038 Bib. Nat. 26r.)

*Of the way to fix in your mind the form of a face*

IF you desire to acquire facility in keeping in your mind the expression of a face, first learn by heart the various different kinds of heads, eyes, noses, mouths, chins, throats, and also necks and shoulders. Take as an instance noses:—they are of ten types: straight, bulbous, hollow, prominent either above or below the centre, aquiline, regular, simian, round, and pointed. These divisions hold good as regards profile. Seen from in front, noses are of twelve types: thick in the middle, thin in the middle, with the tip broad, and narrow at the base, and narrow at the tip, and broad at the base, with nostrils broad or narrow, or high or low, and with the openings either visible or hidden by the tip. And similarly you will find variety in the other features; of which things you ought to make studies from nature and so fix them in your mind. Or when you have to draw a face from memory, carry with you a small note-book in which you have noted down such features, and then when you have cast a glance at the face of the person whom you wish to draw you can look privately and see which nose or mouth has a resemblance to it, and make a tiny mark against it in order to recognise it again at home. Of abnormal faces I here say nothing, for they are kept in mind without difficulty.

*Of the games in which draughtsmen should indulge*

WHEN you, draughtsmen, wish to find some profitable recreation in games you should always practise things which may be of use in your profession, that is by giving your eye accuracy of judgment so that it may know how to estimate the truth as to the length and breadth of objects. So in order to accustom the mind to such things let one of you draw a straight line anywhere on a wall; and then let each of you take a light rush or straw in his hand, and let each cut his own to the length which the first line appears to him when he is distant from it a space of ten braccia, and then let each go up to the copy in order to measure it against the length which he has judged it to be, and he whose measure comes nearest to the length of the copy has done best and is the winner, and he should receive from all the prize which was previously agreed upon by you. Furthermore you should take measurements foreshortened, that is, you should take a spear or some other stick and look before you to a certain point of distance, and then let each set himself to reckon how many times this measure is contained in the said distance. Another thing is to see who can draw the best line one braccio in length, and this may be tested by tightly drawn thread.

Diversions such as these enable the eye to acquire accuracy of judgment, and this is the primary essential of painting.

*Whether it is better to draw in company or no*

I say and am prepared to prove that it is much better to be in the company of others when you draw rather than alone, for many reasons. The first is that you will be ashamed of being seen in the ranks of the draughtsmen if you are outclassed by them, and this feeling of shame will cause you to make progress in study; secondly a rather commendable envy will stimulate you to join the number of those who are more praised than you are, for the praises of the others will serve you as a spur; yet another is that you will acquire something of the manner of anyone whose work is better than yours, while if you are better than the others you will profit by seeing how to avoid their errors, and the praises of others will tend to increase your powers. (ms.2038 Bib. Nat. 26v.)

*Of the proper time for studying the selection of subjects*

THE winter evenings should be spent by youthful students in study of the things prepared during the summer; that is, all the drawings from the nude which you have made in the summer should be brought together, and you should make a choice from among them of the best limbs and bodies, and practise at these and learn them by heart.

*Of attitudes*

AFTERWARDS in the ensuing summer you should make choice of some one who has a good presence, and has not been brought up to wear doublets, and whose figure consequently has not lost its natural bearing, and make him go through various graceful and elegant movements. If he fails to show the muscles very clearly within the outlines of the limbs, this is of no consequence. It is enough for you merely to obtain good attitudes from the figure, and you can correct the limbs by those which you have studied during the winter.

*How it is necessary for the painter to know the inner structure of man*

THE painter who has acquired a knowledge of the nature of the sinews, muscles, and tendons will know exactly in the movement of any limb how many and which of the sinews are the cause of it, and which muscle by its swelling is the cause of this sinew's contracting, and which sinews having been changed into most delicate cartilage surround and contain the said muscle. So he will be able in divers ways and universally to indicate the various muscles by means of the different attitudes of his figures; and he will not do like many who in different actions always make the same things appear in the arm, the back, the breast, and the legs; for such things as these ought not to rank in the category of minor faults.

*Of the choice of beautiful faces*

METHINKS it is no small grace in a painter to be able to give a pleasing air to his figures, and whoever is not naturally possessed of this grace may acquire it by study, as opportunity offers, in the following manner. Be on the watch to take the best parts of many beautiful faces of which the beauty is established rather by general repute than by your own judgment, for you may readily deceive yourself by selecting such faces as bear a resemblance to your own, since it would often seem that such similarities please us; and if you were ugly you would not select beautiful faces, but would be creating ugly faces like many painters whose types often resemble their master; so therefore choose the beautiful ones as I have said, and fix them in your mind. (ms.2038 Bib. Nat. 27r.)

*Of the life of the painter in his studio*

THE painter or draughtsman ought to be solitary, in order that the well-being of the body may not sap the vigour of the mind; and more especially when he is occupied with the consideration and investigation of things which by being continually present before his eyes furnish food to be treasured up in the memory.

If you are alone you belong entirely to yourself; if you are accompanied even by one companion you belong only half to yourself, or even less in proportion to the thoughtlessness of his conduct; and if you have more than one companion you will fall more deeply into the same plight.

If you should say, 'I will take my own course; I will retire apart, so that I may be the better able to investigate the forms of natural objects,' then I say this must needs turn out badly, for you will not be able to prevent yourself from often lending an ear to their chatter; and not being able to serve two masters you will discharge badly the duty of companionship, and even worse that of endeavoring to realise your conceptions in art.

But suppose you say, 'I will withdraw so far apart that their words shall not reach me nor in any way disturb me'. I reply that in this case you will be looked upon as mad, and bear in mind that in so doing you will then be solitary.

If you must have companionship choose it from your studio; it may then help you to obtain the advantages which result from different methods of study. All other companionship may prove extremely harmful.

(ms.2038 Bib. Nat. 27v. and r.)

OF the method of learning aright how to compose groups of figures in historical pictures:

When you have thoroughly learnt perspective, and have fixed in your memory all the various parts and forms of things, you should often amuse yourself when you take a walk for recreation, in watching and taking note of the attitudes and actions of men as they talk and dispute, or laugh or come to blows one with another, both their actions and those of the bystanders who either intervene or stand looking on at these things; noting these down with rapid strokes in this way, in a little pocket-book, which you ought always to carry with you. And let this be of tinted paper, so that it may not be rubbed out; but you should change the old for a new one, for these are not things to be rubbed out but preserved with the utmost diligence; for there is such an infinite number of forms and actions of things that the memory is incapable of preserving them, and therefore you should keep those [sketches] as your patterns and teachers.

*How one ought first to learn diligence rather than rapid execution*

IF as draughtsman you wish to study well and profitably, accustom yourself when you are drawing to work slowly, and to determine between the various lights, which possess the highest degree and measure of brightness, and similarly as to the shadows, which are those that are darker than the rest, and in what manner they mingle together, and to compare their dimensions one with another; and so with the contours to observe which way they are tending, and as to the lines what part of each is curved in one way or another, and where they are more or less conspicuous and consequently thick or fine; and lastly to see that your shadows and lights may blend without strokes or lines in the manner of smoke. And when you shall have trained your hand and judgment with this degree of care it will speedily come to pass that you will have no need to take thought thereto. (ms.2038 Bib. Nat. 27v.)

*Of judging your own picture*

WE know well that mistakes are more easily detected in the works of others than in one's own, and that oftentimes while censuring the small faults of others you will overlook your own great faults. In order to avoid such ignorance make yourself first of all a master of perspective, then gain a complete knowledge of the proportions of man and other animals, and also make yourself a good architect, that is in so far as concerns the form of the buildings and of the other things which are upon the earth, which are infinite in form: and the more knowledge you have of these the more will your work be worthy of praise; and for those things in which you have no practice do not disdain to draw from nature. But to return to what has been promised above, I say that when you are painting you should take a flat mirror and often look at your work within it, and it will then be seen in reverse, and will appear to be by the hand of some other master, and you will be better able to judge of its faults than in any other way.

It is also a good plan every now and then to go away and have a little relaxation; for then when you come back to the work your judgment will be surer, since to remain constantly at work will cause you to lose the power of judgment.

It is also advisable to go some distance away, because then the work appears smaller, and more of it is taken in at a glance, and a lack of harmony or proportion in the various parts and in the colours of the objects is more readily seen.

*This rule ought to be given to children who paint*

WE know clearly that the sight is one of the swiftest actions that can exist, for in the same instant it surveys an infinite number of forms; nevertheless it can only comprehend one thing at a time. To take an instance: you, O Reader, might at a glance look at the whole of this written page, and you would instantly decide that it is full of various letters, but you will not recognise in this space of time either what letters they are or what they purport to say, and therefore it is necessary for you if you wish to gain a knowledge of these letters to take them word by word and line by line.

Again, if you wish to go up to the summit of a building it will be necessary for you to ascend step by step, otherwise it will be impossible to reach the top. So I say to you whom nature inclines to this art that if you would have a true knowledge of the forms of different objects you should commence with their details, and not pass on to the second until the first is well in your memory and you have practised it. If you do otherwise you will be throwing away time, and to a certainty you will greatly prolong the period of study. And remember to acquire diligence rather than facility.

(ms.2038 Bib. Nat. 28r.)

*Of the difference of the measurements in boys and men*

I find a great difference between men and small boys in the length from one joint to another; for whereas the distance from the joint of the shoulder to the elbow, and from the elbow to the tip of the thumb, and from the humerus of one of the shoulders to the other, in a man is twice the head, in a child it is only once, because nature fashions the stature of the seat of the intellect for us before that of its active members.

*Of the rendering of the lights*

MAKE first a general shadow over the whole of the extended part which does not see the light; then give to it the half shadows and the strong shadows, contrasting these one with another.

And similarly give the extended light in half-tone, adding afterwards the half-lights and the high lights and contrasting these in the same manner. (ms.2038 Bib. Nat. 28v.)

IN what way you ought to make a head so that its parts may fit into their true positions:

To make a head so that its features are in agreement with those of a head that turns and bends, use these means: you know that the eyes, eyebrows, nostrils, corners of the mouth and sides of the chin, jaw, cheeks, ears and all the parts of a face are placed at regular positions upon the face, therefore when you have made the face, make lines which pass from one corner of the eye to the other; and so also for the position of each feature. Then having continued the ends of these lines beyond the two sides of the face, observe whether on the right and the left the spaces in the same parallel are equal. But I would specially remind you that you must make these lines extend to the point of your vision.

THE way to represent the eighteen actions of man: [these are] rest, movement, speed; erect, leaning, seated, bending, kneeling, lying down, suspended; carrying, being carried, pushing, dragging, striking, being struck, pressing down and raising up.

YOU will treat first of the lights cast by windows to which you will give the name of restricted light; then treat of the lights of landscape to which you will give the name of restricted light; then treat of the lights of landscape to which you will give the name of free light; then treat of the light of luminous bodies.

*How to make an imaginary animal appear natural*

YOU know that you cannot make any animal without it having its limbs such that each bears some resemblance to that of some one of the other animals. If therefore you wish to make one of your imaginary animals appear natural—let us suppose it to be a dragon—take for its head that of a mastiff or setter, for its eyes those of a cat, for its ears those of a porcupine, for its nose that of a greyhound, with the eyebrows of a lion, the temples of an old cock and the neck of a water-tortoise.

*Of drawing an object*

SEE that when you are drawing and make a beginning of a line, that you look over all the object that you are drawing for any detail whatever which lies in the direction of the line that you have begun. (ms.2038 Bib. Nat. 29r.)

HOW a figure is not worthy of praise unless such action appears in it as serves to express the passion of the soul:

That figure is most worthy of praise which by its action best expresses the passion which animates it.

*How the cast shadow is never equal in size to its cause*

IF as experience shows luminous rays come from a single point, and proceed in the form of a sphere from this point radiating and spreading themselves through the air, the farther they go the more they are dispersed; and an object placed between the light and the wall is always reproduced larger in its shadow, because the rays that strike it have become larger by the time they have reached the wall. (ms.2038 Bib. Nat. 29v.)

*Of the arrangement of the limbs*

AS regards the arrangement of the limbs, you should bear in mind that when you wish to represent one who by some chance has either to turn backwards or on one side, you must not make him move his feet and all his limbs in the same direction as he turns his head; but you should show the process spreading itself and taking effect over the four sets of joints, namely those of the foot, the knee, the hip, and the neck. And if you let his weight rest on the right leg, you should make the knee of the left bend inwards; and the foot of it should be slightly raised on the outside, and the left shoulder should be somewhat lower than the right; and the nape of the neck should be exactly above the outer curve of the ankle of the left foot, and the left shoulder should be above the toe of the right foot in a perpendicular line. And always so dispose your figures that the direction in which the head is turned is not that in which the breast faces, since nature has for our convenience so formed the neck that it can easily serve the different occasions on which the eye desires to turn in various directions; and to this same organ the other joints are in part responsive. And if ever you show a man sitting with his hands at work upon something by his side, make the chest turn upon the hip joints.

*Of the shadow cast by a body situated between two equal lights*

A body which finds itself placed between two equal lights will put forth two shadows, which will take their direction equally according to the lines of the two lights. And if you move the body farther away or bring it nearer to one of the lights, the shadow which points to the nearer light will be less deep than that which points to the one more remote.

*The body nearer to the light will cast the larger shadow, and why*

IF an object placed in front of a particular light be very near to it you will see it cast a very large shadow on the opposite wall, and the farther you remove the object from the light the smaller will the shadow become.

*Why a shadow which is greater than*

THE want of proportion of the shadow which is greater than its cause, arises from the fact that as the light is less than its object it cannot be at an equal distance from the extremities

*its cause will be out of proportion*

of the object, and the part which is at a greater distance increases more than those which are nearer, and therefore the shadow increases.

*Why a shadow which is bigger than the body that causes it has indistinct contours*

ATMOSPHERE which surrounds a light almost partakes of the nature of this light in brightness and in warmth; the farther away it recedes the more it loses this resemblance. An object which casts a large shadow is near to the light and finds itself lit up both by the light and by the luminous atmosphere, and consequently this atmosphere leaves the contours of the shadow indistinct. (ms.2038 Bib. Nat. 30r.)

*How high the point of sight should be placed*

THIS point ought to be at the same level as the eye of an ordinary man; and the end of the flat country which borders upon the sky should be made of the same height as the line where the earth touches the horizon, except for the mountains which are in liberty. (ms.2038 Bib. Nat. 31r.)

*How small figures ought consequently to be left unfinished*

I say that when objects appear of minute size, it is due to the said objects being at a distance from the eye; and when this is the case, there must of necessity be a considerable quantity of atmosphere between the eye and the object, and this atmosphere interferes with the distinctness of the form of the objects, and consequently the minute details of these bodies will become indistinguishable and unrecognisable.

Therefore, O painter, you should make your lesser figures only suggested, and not highly finished; for if you do otherwise, you will produce effects contrary to those of nature, your mistress.

The object is small because of the great space which exists between the eye and it. This great space contains within itself a great quantity of atmosphere; and this atmosphere forms of itself a dense body which interposes and shuts out from the eye the minute details of the objects.

*What background a painter should choose for his works*

SINCE one sees by experience that all bodies are surrounded by shadow and light it is expedient, O painter, that you so dispose the part illuminated that it is outlined against a dark object, and that in the same way the part of the body in shadow is outlined against a bright object. And this rule will be a great help to you in giving relief to your figures.

*Of drawing*

WHEN you have to draw from nature stand three times as far away as the size of the object that you are drawing.

Why does a painting seem better in a mirror than outside it?

*How in all travels one may learn*

THIS benign nature so provides that over all the world you find something to imitate.

*Of shadow*

WHERE the shadow is bounded by light, note carefully where it is lighter or darker, and where it is more or less indistinct towards the light; and above all I would remind you that in youthful figures you should not make the shadows end like stone, for the flesh retains a slight transparency, as may be observed by looking at a hand held between the eye and the sun, when it is seen to flush red and to be of a luminous transparency.

And let the part which is brightest in colour be between the lights and the shadows. And if you wish to see what depth of shadow is needed for the flesh, cast a shadow over it with your finger, and according as you wish it to be lighter or darker, hold your finger nearer or farther away from the picture, and then copy this shadow.

*How one ought to arrange the light upon figures*

THE disposition of the light should be in harmony with the natural conditions under which you represent your figure; that is, if you are representing it in sunlight, make the shadows dark with great spaces of light, and mark the shadows of all the surrounding bodies and their shadows upon the ground. If you represent it in dull weather, make only a slight difference between the lights and the shadows, and do not make any other shadow at the feet. If you represent it within doors, make a strong difference between the lights and shadows and show the shadow on the ground, and, if you represent a window covered by a curtain and the wall white there should be little difference between the lights and shadows. If it is lit by a fire you should make the lights ruddy and powerful and the shadows dark; and the shadows should be sharply defined where they strike the walls or the floor, and the farther away they extend from the body the broader and larger should they become. And if it be lit in part by the fire and in part by the atmosphere, make the part lit by the atmosphere the stronger, and let that lit by the fire be almost as red as fire itself. And above all let the figures that you paint have sufficient light and from above, that is all living persons whom you paint, for the people whom you see in the streets are all lighted from above; and I would have you know that you have no acquaintance so intimate but that if the light fell on him from below you would find it difficult to recognise him.

*The order of learning to draw*

FIRST of all copy drawings by a good master made by his art from nature and not as exercises; then from a relief, keeping by you a drawing done from the same relief; then from a good model; and of this you ought to make a practice.

*At what height the light should be in order to draw from nature*

WHEN you are drawing from nature the light should be from the north, so that it may not vary; and if it is from the south keep the window covered with a curtain so that though the sun shine upon it all day long the light will undergo no change. The elevation of the light should be such that each body casts a shadow on the ground which is of the same length as its height.

*Why beautiful colours should be in the light*

SINCE we see that the quality of colours becomes known by means of light, it is to be inferred that where there is most light there the true quality of the colour so illuminated will be most visible, and where there is most shadow there the colour will be most affected by the colour of the shadow. Therefore, O painter, be mindful to show the true quality of the colours in the parts which are in light.

(ms.2038 Bib. Nat. 33r.)

*Of light and shade*

EACH part of the surface of a body is in part affected by the colour of the thing opposite to it.

*Example*

IF you set a spherical body in the midst of different objects, that is, so that on the one side it has the light of the sun and on the side opposite there is a wall illuminated by the sun, which may be green or some other colour, the surface on which it is resting being red and the two transverse sides dark, you will see the natural colour of this object take on the hues of those colours which are over against it. The strongest will be that proceeding from the light, the second that from the illuminated wall, the third that of the shadow. There yet remains however a portion which will take its hue from the colour of the edges.

THE supreme misfortune is when theory outstrips performance.

IN the choice of figures aim at softness and delicacy rather than that they should be stiff and wooden.

*Of small lights*

THE lights cast from small windows also present a strong contrast of light and shadow, more especially if the chamber lit by them is large; and this is not good to use in painting.
(ms.2038 Bib. Nat. 33v.)

THE painter who draws by practice and judgment of the eye without the use of reason, is like the mirror that reproduces within itself all the objects which are set opposite to it without knowledge of the same. (C.A. 76r.a)

THAT countenance which in a picture is looking full in the face of the master who makes it will always be looking at all the spectators. And the figure painted when seen below from above will always appear as though seen below from above, although the eye of the beholder may be lower than the picture itself. (C.A. 111v.b)

*Of the parts of the face*

IF nature had only one fixed standard for the proportions of the various parts, then the faces of all men would resemble each other to such a degree that it would be impossible to distinguish one from another; but she has varied the five parts of the face in such a way that although she has made an almost universal standard as to their size, she has not observed it in the various conditions to such a degree as to prevent one from being clearly distinguished from another. (C.A. 119v.a)

AS the body with great slowness produced by the length of its contrary movement turns in greater space and thereby gives a stouter blow, whereas movements which are continuous and short have little strength—so study upon the same subject made at long intervals of time causes the judgment to become more perfect and the better to recognise its own mistakes. And the same is true of the eye of the painter as it draws farther away from his picture. (C.A. 122v.a)

A picture or any representation of figures ought to be done in such a way that those who see them may be able with ease to recognise from their attitudes what is passing through their minds. So if you have to represent a man of good repute in the act of speaking, make his gestures accord with the probity of his speech; and similarly if you have to represent a brutal man, make him with fierce movements flinging out his arms towards his hearer, and the head and chest protruding forward beyond the feet should seem to accompany the hands of the speaker.

Just so a deaf mute who sees two people talking, although being himself deprived of the power of hearing, is none the less able to divine from the movements and gestures of the speakers the subject of their discussion.

I once saw in Florence a man who had become deaf, who could not understand you if you spoke to him loudly, while if you spoke softly without letting the voice utter any sound, he understood you merely from the movement of the lips. Perhaps, however, you will say to me: 'But does not a man who speaks loudly move his lips like one who speaks softly? And since the one moves his lips like the other, will not the one be understood like the other?' As to this I leave the decision to the test of experience. Set someone to speak softly and then [louder], and watch the lips. (C.A. 139r.d)

HOW from age to age the art of painting continually declines and deteriorates when painters have no other standard than work already done:

The painter will produce pictures of little merit if he takes the works of others as his standard; but if he will apply himself to learn from the objects of nature he will produce good results. This we see was the case with the painters who came after the time of the Romans, for they continually imitated each other, and from age to age their art steadily declined.

After these came Giotto the Florentine, and he—reared in mountain solitudes, inhabited only by goats and such like beasts—turning straight from nature to his art, began to draw on the rocks the movements of the goats which he was tending, and so began to draw the figures of all the animals which were to be found in the country, in such a way that after much study he not only surpassed the masters of his own time but all those of many preceding centuries. After him art again declined, because all were imitating paintings already done; and so for centuries it continued to decline until such time as Tommaso the Florentine; nicknamed Masaccio, showed by the perfection of his work how those who took as their standard anything other than nature, the supreme guide of all the masters, were wearying themselves in vain. Similarly I would say about these mathematical subjects, that those who study only the authorities and not the works of nature are in art the grandsons and not the sons of nature, which is the supreme guide of the good authorities.

Mark the supreme folly of those who censure such as learn from nature, leaving uncensured the authorities who were themselves the disciples of this same nature! (C.A. 141r.b)

*Painting*

THE surface of each body takes part of the colour of whatever is set against it. The colours of the objects in light are reproduced on each other's surface at different spots according to the varieties in the positions of these objects. . . . Let *o* be a blue object in light, which alone by itself faces the space *b c* of the white sphere *a b c d e f,* and tinges it blue; and let *m* be a yellow object which is reflected on the space *a b* in company with the blue object *o,* and tinges it green, by the second of this which shows that blue and yellow together produces a most beautiful green, etc.—and the rest will be set forth in the Book on Painting. In that book it will be demonstrated, by transmitting the images of the bodies and colours of the things illuminated by the sun through a small round hole in a dark place on to a smooth surface which in itself is white. But everything will be upside down. (C.A. 181r.a)

*The life of the painter in the country*

THE painter requires such knowledge of mathematics as belongs to painting, and severance from companions who are not in sympathy with his studies, and his brain should have the power of adapting itself to the tenor of the objects which present themselves before it, and he should be freed from all other cares.

And if while considering and examining one subject a second should intervene, as happens when an object occupies the mind, he ought to decide which of these subjects presents greater difficulties in investigation, and follow that until it becomes entirely clear, and afterwards pursue the investigation of the other. And above all he should keep his mind as clear as the surface of a mirror, which becomes changed to as many different colours as are those of the object within it, and his companions should resemble him in a taste for these studies, and if he fail to find any such he should accustom himself to be alone in his investigations, for in the end he will find no more profitable companionship. (C.A. 184v.c)

*Of the order to be observed in study*

I say that one ought first to learn about the limbs and how they are worked, and after having completed this knowledge one ought to study their actions in the different conditions in which men are placed, and thirdly to devise figure compositions, the studies for these being taken from natural actions made on occasion as opportunities offered; and one should be on the watch in the streets and squares and fields, and there make sketches with rapid strokes to represent features, that is for a head one may make an *o,* and for an arm a straight or curved line, and so in like manner for the legs and trunk, afterwards when back at home working up these notes in a completed form.

My opponent says that in order to gain experience and to learn how to work readily, it is better that the first period of study should be spent in copying various compositions made by different masters either on sheets of paper or on walls, since from these one acquires rapidity in execution and a good method. But to this it may be replied that the ensuing method would be good if it was founded upon works that were excellent in composition and by diligent masters; and since such masters are so rare that few are to be found, it is safer to go direct to the works of nature than to those which have been imitated from her originals with great deterioration and thereby to acquire a bad method, for he who has access to the fountain does not go to the water-pot. (C.A. 199v.a)

THESE rules are to be used solely in testing figures; for every man in his first compositions makes certain mistakes, and if he does not become conscious of them he does not correct them; therefore in order to discover mistakes you should test your work and where you find there mistakes correct them, and remember never to fall into them again. But if you were to attempt to apply all these rules in composition you would never make a beginning and would cause confusion in your work.

These rules are intended to help you to a free and good judgment; for good judgment proceeds from good understanding, and good understanding comes from reason trained by good rules, and good rules are the children of sound experience, which is the common mother of all the sciences, and arts. If therefore you bear well in mind the precepts of my rules you will be able merely by the accuracy of your judgment to criticize and discern every error in proportion in any work, whether it is in the perspective or in the figures or other things. (C.A. 221v.d)

ALL the limbs of every kind of animal should correspond with its age, that is, the young should not show their veins or nerves as most [painters] do in order to show their dexterity in art, spoiling the whole by mistakes in the limbs.

ALL the parts of an animal should correspond with the whole, that is, when a man is short and thickset you must see that each of his limbs is short and thickset.

LET the movements of men be such as are in keeping with their dignity or meanness. (C.A. 345v.b)

MAKE your work to be in keeping with your purpose and design; that is, when you make your figure you should consider carefully who it is and what you wish it to be doing.

In order to produce an effect of similar action in a picture of an old man and a young, you must make the action of the young man appear more vigorous in proportion as he is more powerful than the old man, and you will make the same difference between a young man and an infant.

IF you have to represent a man either as moving or lifting or pulling, or carrying a weight equal to his own weight, how ought you to fit the legs under his body? (C.A. 349r.b)

PAINTERS oftentimes deceive themselves by representing water in which they render visible what is seen by man; whereas the water sees the object from one side and the man sees it from the other; and it frequently happens that the painter will see a thing from above and the water sees it from beneath, and so the same body is seen in front and behind, and above and below, for the water reflects the image of the object in one way and the eye sees it in another. (C.A. 354r.d)

WE consider as a monstrosity one who has a very large head and short legs, and as a monstrosity also one who is in great poverty and has rich garments; we should therefore deem him well proportioned in whom the parts are in harmony with the whole. (C.A. 375r.c)

*Of the error which is committed in judging as to the limbs*

THE painter who has clumsy hands will reproduce the same in his works, and the same thing will happen with every limb unless long study prevents it. Do you then, O painter, take careful note of that part in yourself which is most mis-shapen and apply yourself by study to remedy this entirely. For if you are brutal, your figures will be the same and devoid of grace, and in like manner every quality that there is within you of good or of evil will be in part revealed in your figures. (A 23r.)

WHEN you draw nudes be careful always to draw the whole figure, and then finish the limb which seems the best and at the same time study its relation to the other limbs, as otherwise you may form the habit of never properly joining the limbs together.

Take care never to make the head turn the same way as the chest nor the arm move with the leg; and if the head is turned toward the right shoulder make all the parts lower on the left side than on the right, but if you make the chest prominent and the head turning on the left side, then make the parts on the right side higher than those on the left. (A 28v.)

NOTE in the movements and attitudes of the figures how the limbs and their expression vary, because the shoulder blades in the movements of the arms and shoulders alter considerably the position of the back bone; and you will find all the causes of this in my book of Anatomy.

*Of shadows and lights*

YOU, who reproduce the works of nature, behold the dimensions, the degrees of intensity, and the forms of the lights and shadows of each muscle, and observe in the lengths of their figures towards which muscle they are directed by the axis of their central lines. (E 3r.)

*Of the background of the figures in painting*

THE background that surrounds the figures in any subject composition ought to be darker than the illuminated part of these figures, and lighter than their part in shadow. (E 4r.)

THAT every part of a whole should be in proportion to its whole: thus if a man has a thick short figure that he should be the same in every one of his limbs, that is, with short thick arms, big hands, fingers thick and short, with joints of the same character and so with the rest. And I would have the same understood to apply to all kinds of animals and plants; thus, in diminishing the parts, do so in proportion to their size, as also in enlarging.

*Of how to paint wind*

IN representing wind, in addition to showing the bending of the boughs and the inverting of their leaves at the approach of the wind, you should represent the clouds of fine dust mingled with the troubled air. (E 6v.)

*Of the requisites of painting*

THE first requisite of painting is that the bodies which it represents should appear in relief, and that the scenes which surround them with effects of distance should seem to enter into the plane in which the picture is produced by means of the three parts of perspective, namely the diminution in the distinctness of the form of bodies, the diminution in their size, and the diminution in their colour. Of these three divisions of perspective, the first has its origin in the eye, the two others are derived from the atmosphere that is interposed between the eye and the objects which the eye beholds.

The second requisite of painting is that the actions should be appropriate and have a variety in the figures, so that the men may not all look as though they were brothers. (E 79v.)

*Of variety in figures*

THE painter ought to strive at being universal, for there is a great lack of dignity in doing one thing well and another badly, like many who study only the measurements and proportions of the nude figure and do not seek after its variety; for a man may be properly proportioned and yet be fat and short or long and thin, or medium. And whoever does not take count of these varieties will always make his figures in one mould, so that they will all appear sisters, and this practice deserves severe censure.

*Of the order of acquiring this universality*

IT is an easy matter for whoever knows how to represent man to afterwards acquire this universality, for all the animals which live upon the earth resemble each other in their limbs, that is in muscles, sinews and bones, and they do not vary at all, except in length or thickness as will be shown in the Anatomy. There are also the aquatic animals, of which there are many different kinds; but with regard to these I do not advise the painter to make a fixed standard, for they are of almost infinite variety; and the same is also true of the insect world. (G 5v.)

*Of the error made by those who practise without science* [1]

THOSE who are enamoured of practice without science are like a pilot who goes into a ship without rudder or compass and never has any certainty where he is going.

Practice should always be based upon a sound knowledge of theory, of which perspective is the guide and gateway, and without it nothing can be done well in any kind of painting. (G 8r.)

OF the lights on the lower extremities of bodies packed tightly together, such as men in battle:

Of men and horses labouring in battle, the different parts should be darker in proportion as they are closer to the ground on which they are supported; and this is proved from the sides of wells, which become darker in proportion to their depth, this being due to the fact that the lowest part of the well sees and is seen by a lesser amount of the luminous atmosphere than any other part of it. And the pavements when they are the same colour as the legs of the men and horses will always seem in higher light within equal angles than will these same legs. (G 15r.)

*How to pass judgment upon a painter's work*

FIRST you should consider the figures whether they have the relief which their position requires, and the light that illuminates them, so that the shadows may not be the same at the extremities of the composition as in the centre, because it is one thing for a figure to be surrounded by shadows, and another for it to have the shadows only on one side. Those figures are surrounded by shadows which are towards the centre of the composition, because they are shaded by the dark figures interposed between them and the light; and those are shaded on one side only which are interposed between the light and the main group, for where they do not face the light they face the group, and there they reproduce the darkness cast by this group, and where they do not face the group they face the brightness of the light, and there they reproduce its radiance.

Secondly, you should consider whether the distribution or arrangement of the figures is devised in agreement with the conditions you desire the action to represent.

Thirdly, whether the figures are actively engaged on their purpose. (G 19r.)

*Of painting*

A very important part of painting consists in the backgrounds of the things painted. Against these backgrounds the contour lines of such natural bodies as possess convex curves will always reveal the shapes of these bodies, even though the colours of the bodies are of the same hue as the background.

This arises from the fact of the convex boundaries of the objects not being illuminated in the same manner as the background is by the same light, because frequently the contours are clearer or darker than the background.

Should however these contours be of the same colour as the background, then undoubtedly this part of the picture will interfere with the perception of the figure formed by these contour lines. Such a predicament in painting ought to be avoided by the judgment of good painters, since the painter's intention is to make his bodies appear detached from the background; and in the above-mentioned instance the contrary occurs, not only in the painting but in the objects in relief. (G 23v.)

*An indication whether a youth has an aptitude for painting*

THERE are many men who have a desire and love for drawing but no aptitude for it, and this can be discerned in children if they are not diligent and never finish their copies with shading.

The painter is not worthy of praise who does only one thing well, as the nude, or a head, or draperies, or animal life, or landscapes, or such other special subject; for there is no one so dull of understanding that after devoting himself to one subject only and continually practising at this, he will fail to do it well. (G 25r.)

[*The representation of things in movement*]
OF the imitation of things which though they have movement in their own place, do not in this movement reveal themselves as they are in reality.

Drops of water when it rains, a winder, the turning-wheel, stones under the action of water, firebrands whirled round in a circle, proceed continuously, among things which are not in continuous movement. (G 35r.)

*Of painting*

THE high lights or the lustre of any particular object will not be situated in the centre of the illuminated part, but will make as many changes of position as the eye that beholds it. (H 90 [42]v.)

PAINTERS have a good opportunity of observing actions in players, especially at ball or tennis or with the mallet when they are contending together, better indeed than in any other place or exercise. (I 48v.)

IT is the extremities of all things which impart to them grace or lack of grace. (I 92 [44]v.)

MEN and words are actual, and you, painter, if you do not know how to execute your figures, will be like an orator who does not know how to use his words. (K 110 [30]v.)

IT is a necessary thing for the painter, in order to be able to fashion the limbs correctly in the positions and actions which they can represent in the nude, to know the anatomy of the sinews, bones, muscles and tendons in order to know, in the various different movements and impulses, which sinew or muscle is the cause of each movement, and to make only these prominent and thickened, and not the others all over the limb, as do many who in order to appear great draughtsmen make their nudes wooden and without grace, so that it seems rather as if you were looking at a sack of nuts than a human form or at a bundle of radishes rather than the muscles of nudes. (L 79r.)

IN all things seen one has to consider three things, namely

the position of the eye that sees, the position of the object seen and the position of the light that illumines this body.

(M 80r.)

[*With sketch*]

IN the last folds of the joints of any limb everything which was in relief becomes a hollow, and similarly every hollow in the last of the said folds is changed into a protuberance when the end of the limb is straightened.

He who has not a knowledge of this, often makes very great mistakes through relying too much upon his own skill, and not having recourse to the imitation of nature. And such variation is found more in the middle of the sides than in front and more behind than at the sides. (B.M. 44r.)

THE painter contends with and rivals nature.

(*Forster* III 44v.)

[*On draperies*]

ON the thin clothes of the women in walking, running and jumping, and their variety.

[*Notes on painting*]

AND in painting make a discourse on the clothes and other raiments.

And you, O painter, who desire to perform great things, know that unless you first learn to do them well and with good foundations, the work that you do will bring you very little honour and less gain, but if you do it well it will produce you plenty of honour and be of great utility.

(*Quaderni* IV 15r.)

WHEN the subject of your picture is a history make two points, one of the eye and the other of the light, and make the latter as far distant as possible. (*Windsor: Drawings* 12604r.)

NATURE of movements in man. Do not repeat the same actions in the limbs of men unless the necessity of their action constrains you. (*Windsor: Drawings* 19149v.)

*Of colours*

OF colours of equal whiteness that will seem most dazzling which is on the darkest background, and black will seem most intense when it is against a background of greater whiteness.

Red also will seem most vivid when against a yellow

background, and so in like manner with all the colours when set against those which present the sharpest contrasts.
(C.A. 184v.c.)

*Painting*

COLOURS seen in shadow will reveal more or less of their natural beauty in proportion as they are in fainter or deeper shadow.

But if the colours happen to be in a luminous space they will show themselves of greater beauty in proportion as the luminosity is more intense.

### *Adversary*

THE varieties in the colours of shadows are as numerous as the varieties in colour of the objects which are in the shadows.

### *Reply*

COLOURS seen in shadow will reveal less variety one with another according as the shadows wherein they lie are deeper. There is evidence of this from those who from a space without peer within the doorways of shadowy temples, for there the pictures clad as they are in divers colours all seem robed in darkness.

So therefore at a long distance all the shadows of different colours appear of the same darkness.

Of bodies clad in light and shade it is the illuminated part which reveals the true colour. (E 18r.)

*Painting*

SINCE white is not a colour but is capable of becoming the recipient of every colour, when a white object is seen in the open air all its shadows are blue; and this comes about in accordance with the fourth proposition, which says that the surface of every opaque body partakes of the colour of surrounding objects. As therefore this white object is deprived of the light of the sun by the interposition of some object which comes between the sun and it, all that portion of it which is exposed to the sun and the atmosphere continues to partake of the colour of the sun and the atmosphere, and that part which is not exposed to the sun remains in shadow, and partakes only of the colour of the atmosphere.

And if this white object should neither reflect the green of the fields which stretch out to the horizon nor yet face the brightness of the horizon itself, it would undoubtedly appear of such simple colour as the atmosphere showed itself to be. (F 75r.)

*Of painting in the country*

IF between the eye and the horizon there intervenes the slope of a hill that drops towards the eye, and the eye finds itself at about the middle of the height of the slope then the hill will acquire darkness with every stage of its length. This is proved by the seventh of this which says; that plant will show itself darker which is seen more below; therefore the proposition is confirmed, because the hill shows from the centre downwards all its plants in the parts which are as much illumined by the brightness of the sky, as the part which is in shade is shaded by the darkness of the earth. For which reason it is necessary that these plants should be of moderate darkness, and from this point on towards the bases of the hills the plants are continually becoming brighter through the converse of the seventh proposition, for by this seventh proposition the nearer such plants are to the summit of the hill the more of necessity they become darker. And it follows that this darkness is not proportionate to the distance, from the eighth proposition which says: that thing will show itself darker which finds itself in finer air; and by the tenth: that will show itself darker which borders on the brighter background. (C.A. 184v.c)

HOW painting surpasses all human works by reason of the subtle possibilities which it contains:

The eye, which is called the window of the soul, is the chief means whereby the understanding may most fully and abundantly appreciate the infinite works of nature; and the ear is the second, inasmuch as it acquires its importance from the fact that it hears the things which the eye has seen. If you historians, or poets, or mathematicians had never seen things with your eyes you would be ill able to describe them in your writings. And if you, O poet, represent a story by depicting it with your pen, the painter with his brush will so render it as to be more easily satisfying and less tedious to understand. If you call painting 'dumb poetry', then the painter may say of the poet that his art is 'blind painting'.

Consider then which is the more grievous affliction, to be blind or to be dumb! Although the poet has as wide a choice of subjects as the painter, his creations fail to afford as much satisfaction to mankind as do paintings, for while poetry attempts to represent forms, actions and scenes with words, the painter employs the exact images of these forms in order to reproduce them. Consider, then, which is more fundamental to man, the name of man or his image? The name changes with change of country; the form is unchanged except by death.

And if the poet serves the understanding by way of the ear, the painter does so by the eye, which is the nobler sense.

I will only cite as an instance of this how if a good painter represents the fury of a battle and a poet also describes one, and the two descriptions are shown together to the public, you will soon see which will draw most of the spectators, and where there will be most discussion, to which most praise will be given and which will satisfy the more. There is no doubt that the painting, which is by far the more useful and beautiful, will give the greater pleasure. Inscribe in any place the name of God and set opposite to it His image, you will see which will be held in greater reverence!

Since painting embraces within itself all the forms of nature, you have omitted nothing except the names, and these are not universal like the forms. If you have the results of her processes we have the processes of her results.

Take the case of a poet describing the beauties of a lady to her lover and that of a painter who makes a portrait of her; you will see whither nature will the more incline the enamoured judge. Surely the proof of the matter ought to rest upon the verdict of experience!

You have set painting among the mechanical arts! Truly were painters as ready equipped as you are to praise their own works in writing, I doubt whether it would endure the reproach of so vile a name. If you call it mechanical because it is by manual work that the hands represent what the imagination creates, your writers are setting down with the pen by manual work what originates in the mind. If you call it mechanical because it is done for money, who fall into this error—if indeed it can be called an error—more than you yourselves? If you lecture for the Schools do you not go to whoever pays you the most? Do you do any work without some reward?

And yet I do not say this in order to censure such opinions, for every labour looks for its reward. And if the poet should say, 'I will create a fiction which shall express great things', so likewise will the painter also, for even so Apelles made the Calumny. If you should say that poetry is the more enduring,—to this I would reply that the works of a coppersmith are more enduring still, since time preserves them longer than either your works or ours; nevertheless they show but little imagination; and painting, if it be done upon copper in enamel colours, can be made far more enduring.

In Art we may be said to be grandsons unto God. If poetry treats of moral philosophy, painting has to do with natural philosophy; if the one describes the workings of the mind, the other considers what the mind effects by movements of the body; if the one dismays folk by hellish fictions, the other does the like by showing the same things in action. Suppose the poet sets himself to represent some image of beauty or terror, something vile and foul, or some monstrous thing, in contest with the painter, and suppose in his own way he makes a change of forms at his pleasure, will not the painter still satisfy the more? Have we not seen pictures which bear so close a resemblance to the actual thing that they have deceived both men and beasts?

If you know how to describe and write down the appearance of the forms, the painter can make them so that they appear enlivened with lights and shadows which create the very expression of the faces; herein you cannot attain with the pen where he attains with the brush.

(ms.2038 Bib. Nat. 19r. and v., 20r.)

# MICHELANGELO

*FRANCISCO DE HOLLANDA, who was born in Portugal about 1517 and died in 1584, was Dutch by origin, as his name indicates. He learned the arts of drawing, illuminating, and modeling under his father, Antonio, and lived in the humanist milieu that surrounded Dom Affonso, the learned young bishop of the Portuguese town of Evora. Drawn by Italy, Francisco went there in 1537 as an official agent of King John III. Immediately on arriving in Rome, he set about to court the friendship of Michelangelo, who reigned as master of the art of his time. By then Michelangelo had painted the ceiling of the Sistine Chapel and sculptured his "Moses" and the tombs of the Medicis, and was at work on his fresco of the Last Judgment. The church of Saint Sylvester was the setting for the meetings of Michelangelo, his mistress, Vittoria Colonna, and the young Portuguese. It is generally agreed that the transcriptions of Michelangelo's words that Francisco set down in his* Four Dialogues on Painting *are faithful. The great painter rarely expressed himself on painting in his writings, and for this reason Francisco de Hollanda's work is enormously valuable to us. From these interveiws we have selected the pages in which Michelangelo expounds his most fertile ideas. He sometimes contradicts Da Vinci. Michelangelo denies that painting has a scientific character, and appears to be a traditionalist. As a sculptor, he defends sculpture, subordinating painting to it; as a painter, he rejects nature, exalting the plastic representation of the human form rather than the reproduction of landscapes.*

## *Dialogues on Painting*

WHEN I arrived at San Silvestro, Frà Ambrogio's lecture on the Epistles was over and he had gone away, and they were beginning to complain of me and my lateness. After I had begged and received pardon for my tardiness and the Signora Marchesa had teased me a little and I in turn had teased Michael Angelo, I asked permission to resume our conversation about painting and proceeded to say:

I think, Signor Michael Angelo, that last Sunday, when we were going away, you said to me that if in Portugal, which you here call Spain, they were to see the noble paintings of Italy, they would hold them in high honour. I would therefore beg this favour of your Worship (since for no other favours came I to Italy), that you would deign to inform me what celebrated paintings there are in Italy, that I may know which I have already seen and what remain for me to see.

It is a great matter that you ask, Messer Francisco, said Michael Angelo, and long and difficult to answer fully; for it is well known that there is no prince or private person or nobleman of any pretensions in Italy, however little curious he be (setting aside those excellent men who adore painting), who does not endeavour to own some fragment of divine painting, or else orders many works of such painting as they can obtain; and thus a good part of its loveliness lies scattered in the noble cities, fortresses, country houses, palaces, and temples and other private and public buildings. But although I have not seen all of them thoroughly, I shall be able to speak of some of the principal ones. At Siena there is notable painting in the town hall and elsewhere. At Florence, my native town, in the palace of the Medici there is a grotesque by Giovanni da Udine; and so throughout Tuscany. At Urbino the palace of the duke, who was himself half a painter, contains much excellent work; and the country house near Pessaro, called Villa Imperiale, built by his wife, is magnificently painted. Likewise the palace of the Duke of Mantua, where Andrea [Mantegna] painted the Triumph of Julius Caesar, is noble, and even more so the stables, painted by Giulio [Clovio] (a disciple of Raffaele), who now flourishes at Mantua. At Ferrara we have the painting of Dosso [Dossi] in the palace of the Castle, and at Padua the loggia by Messer Luigi [Capponi?] is praised, as is the fortress of Legnago. At Venice there are admirable works by the Cavalliere Tiziano, who excels in painting and in portraits; some of them in the library of St. Mark and others in the Fondaco dei Tedeschi. Others there are by good painters in the churches, and the whole of that city is a good painting. There is good work, too, at Pisa and Lucca, at Bologna, Piacenza,

Parma, where Parmigianino is, Milan, and Naples. At Genoa there is the house of Prince Doria, painted by Messer Perino [del Vaga] very ably, especially the storm of the ships of Aeneas, painted in oil, and the fierceness of Neptune and his sea-horses; and in another room there is a fresco showing the war waged at Phlegra between the giants and Jupiter, who is hurling them to the earth with thunderbolts; and almost the whole of the city is a painting, inside and out. And in many other fortresses and towns of Italy, as at Orvieto, Esi, Ascoli, Como, there are panels of noble painting of high worth (I only mention such). And to speak of the paintings and pictures owned by private persons and in each case held dearer than life were an endless task. And you will find some cities of Italy which are painted almost all over, with tolerably good painting, inside and outside the houses.

Messer Michael seemed to make an end of speaking, and the Signora Marchesa, looking at me, said:

Do you notice, Messer Francisco, how Messer Michael has omitted to speak of Rome, so as not to speak of his own work? Let us then do for him what he refused to do for himself, in order to embarrass him the more; since when one speaks of celebrated painting none other has any value beside the fountain-head from which they all spring and have their being. And this is in the fountain-head of the Church, I mean the church of St. Peter's at Rome; the frescoes of a great barrel-vaulted ceiling with its arches and façade, whereon Michael Angelo has divinely pictured how God first made the world, divided into subjects, with many images of sibyls and figures of consummate art and beauty. And it is very notable that this vault, his only work, which he has not yet finished although he began it when a youth, in itself contains the work of twenty painters in one. The second masterpiece in this city, such that it would be the first were it not for the work of Michael Angelo, was painted by Raffaele of Urbino; the frescoes of three stanze and a loggia in the palace of this same St. Peter's, a magnificent work, of well-chosen subjects executed with admirable discretion; noteworthy especially is the subject of Apollo playing on his harp among the nine Muses on Parnassus. In the house of Agostino Guis [Chigi] Raffaele painted with charming poetry the story of

Psyche and delightfully surrounded Galatea with marine monsters in the sea and with cupids in the air. The picture of the Transfiguration in oil at San Pietro in Montorio is very good, as is another at Aracoeli and a fresco in the church of Santa Maria della Pace. The painting of the Venetian Sebastiano [del Piombo] in San Pietro in Montorio, done to compete with Raffaele, is famous. By the architect Baldassare [Peruzzi] of Siena there are many fronts of palaces in this city, in black and white, and by Marturino, and Polidoro [da Caravaggio], a man who in that style magnificently adorned Rome. And there are here many other palaces of cardinals and others, adorned in grotesque and in stucco and in many other different ways, for it is the most painted city in the whole world, apart from pictures owned by private persons, each of whom holds them 'dearer than his life'. Of things outside the city, the Vigna [Giulia], begun by Pope Clement VII at the foot of Monte Mario, is most worth seeing, adorned as it is with fine painting by Raffaele and Giulio [Clovio], where is the sleeping giant whose feet the satyrs are measuring with their crooks. Consider then if these be works to pass over in silence in our city.

She was ceasing to speak when I bethought me and said:

And indeed your Excellency has omitted the remarkable tomb or chapel of the Medici at San Lorenzo in Florence, painted [in marble] by Michael Angelo with such mighty statues in full relief that it may well rival any work of the ancients; in which the goddess or likeness of Night, lying asleep on a bird of night, gave me most pleasure, and the melancholy of a dead man who appeared to live, albeit there is much other noble sculpture there around the Dawn.

But I cannot keep silence about a work of painting which I saw, although it was not in Italy but in France, in Provence in the city of Avignon at a monastery of St. Francis; it was the picture of a dead woman who had been very beautiful and was known as the fair Anne; and a King of France who enjoyed painting and himself painted, called, if I mistake not, Reynel [René], on a visit to Avignon inquired if the fair Anne was there, as he greatly wished to see her and paint her portrait; and when they told him that she had died not long since, he had her disinterred, to see if her bones would give any indication of her beauty. He found her in an old-fashioned dress, her gold hair wound about her head, as though she were alive, but all the fair beauty of her face, which alone he had uncovered, transformed into a skull; and even so the painter-king considered her so beautiful that he painted her portrait, and set many verses round it to mourn her, as they still do to this day. That work I saw in that place and it seemed to me not unworthy of mention in this.

They were much pleased with my picture, and Michael Angelo added that I would also have seen at Narbonne the painting of Sebastiano [del Piombo] in the cathedral; and I went on:

France, too, has some good painting, and the king of France has many palaces and pleasure-houses which contain countless pictures; as at Fontainebleau, where for a long period he kept two hundred well-paid painters at work, and at 'Madrid', the pleasure-house which he built and in which he sometimes imprisons himself of his own free will, in memory of the Spanish Madrid, where he was a prisoner.

I think, said Messer Lattanzio, that I heard Francisco de Hollanda just now include among works of painting the tomb which you, Signor Michael, carved in marble; and I know not how you may give to sculpture the name of painting.

Then I began to laugh aloud, and, craving permission of the master, I said:

In order to save Signor Michael trouble, I will answer this doubt of Signor Lattanzio's, which has followed me hither from my own country. As you will find that all the professions which have most art and understanding and charm are those most nearly akin to the design in painting, so those which are nearest it proceed from it and are parts or members of it, as sculpture or the carving of statues, which is naught else but the very art of painting; for though to some it appear a separate art, yet is it condemned to serve painting, its mistress. And the best proof of this, as your Excellencies will know better than I, is that in books we find Phidias and Praxiteles celebrated as painters, although we know for certain that they were sculptors in marble and see the stone statues from their hand close to us on this very hill, I mean the horses which they made and which King Tiridates sent as a present to Nero, whence the modern name of Monte Cavallo. And if that is not enough, I will say that Donatello (whom I beg leave of Signor Michael to call the first modern sculptor to deserve fame and renown in Italy) in instructing his pupils used merely to bid them draw and would sum up all his teaching in the phrase: 'My pupils, when I bid you draw I give you the whole art of sculpture.' And this is stated by Pomponius Gauricus in his book *De Re Statuaria.*

But why go far in search of proofs and examples which are perhaps close at hand? For, not to speak of myself, I say that the great draughtsman Michael Angelo here present carves also in marble, although that is not his profession, and does so better, if one might say so, than he paints with a brush on wood; and he himself has told me several times that he finds carving in stone less difficult than the use of colours and considers it a far greater thing to make a masterly stroke with a brush than with a chisel. But a celebrated draughtsman will, if he so wish, be able to sculpture and carve in hard marble and bronze and silver huge statues in full relief (a thing difficult to achieve) without having ever previously taken a chisel in his hand, owing to his great skill and strength in draughtsmanship and design. On the other hand the sculptor will not be able to paint nor take a brush in his hand nor as painter make a single stroke of a great master, as I realized the other day on a visit to Baccio Blandino [Bandinello], for I found him attempting to paint in oils and unable to do so. The draughtsman will have skill at once to build palaces and temples and to carve statues and to paint pictures; for Signor Michael himself and Raffaele and Baldassare [Peruzzi] of Siena, famous painters, taught both architecture and sculpture, and Baldassare, after brief study of that art, could rival Bramante, that most eminent architect, who had devoted his whole life to it and who even said that he excelled him in wealth of invention and in splendour and boldness of design. I am speaking of true painters only.

I say moreover, Messer Lattanzio, said Michael, in support of Messer Francisco, that the painter of whom he speaks will not only be instructed in the liberal arts and sciences appertaining to architecture and sculpture, that is, to his own profession, but in all other manual arts throughout the world he will, if he choose, excel even those who profess them. Indeed I sometimes think and imagine that I can find among men but one art or science, that of drawing or painting, from which all the rest branch out. For if one considers well all that is done in this life, one will find that every man unconsciously is engaged in painting this world, both in creating and producing new forms and figures, in dressing variously, in building and filling in spaces with buildings and houses, in cultivating the fields and ploughing the land into sketches and pictures, in sailing over the sea, in fighting and ordering an armed host, and finally in deaths and funerals and all other movements, actions, and occasions. I do not mention the arts and professions of which painting is the fountainhead, some of which are rivers flowing from it, as sculpture and architecture, others mere streams, as the mechanical arts, and some are stagnant pools, as the cutting out with scissors and other useless devices; and all flow from that great flood which in ancient days overwhelmed all things in its might, as is seen in the works of the Romans, which all spring from the art of painting. For in all their painted buildings and constructions, in their works in gold and other metals, in all their vases and ornaments, even in their delicately cut coins, in their dress, their arms, their triumphs, and all their other works and actions one may easily see that, when they were masters of the world, the art of painting was universal ruler and mistress of all works and arts and sciences, including even writing and the composition of history. So that all human actions, if they be considered with understanding, will without doubt be found to be either painting or some part of painting; but although the painter will have skill to invent what was not previously known and to work at all other professions with much more cunning charm of style than the very men who profess them, yet cannot any of those others become a true painter or draughtsman.

I am satisfied, answered Lattanzio, and realize better the great power of painting which, as you have mentioned, is seen in all the works of the ancients, even in their writing and composition. And wrapped in your great conceptions you may not have noticed, as I have, the great conformity between letters and painting (that of painting with letters you certainly will have noted); and that these two arts are such twin sisters that neither of them is perfect apart from the other, although at the present day they appear to some extent separate. Nevertheless any learned man versed in any science will find that in all his works he is always following in many ways the art of a cunning painter, setting forth the colour and shades of his meaning with great care and skill. If we open ancient books, there are few of the celebrated among them but will seem to be pictures and painting; and the reason why some of them are heavy and confused is simply that the author was not a good draughtsman and skilled in the design and proportion of his work; and those which are of easier, more concise style are the work of a better draughtsman. Indeed Quintilian in his consummate work on Rhetoric would have his orator not only draw up his words in their due order but actually learn the art of drawing and sketching. And the more one finds that painting and writing were both called painting, or in the time of Demosthenes antigraphy, which means drawing or writing and was a word used indifferently of both these arts; and that the writing of Agatharcus may be called the painting of Agatharcus. And among the Egyptians, too, I think that those who had to write or describe anything were all painters, for their very hieroglyphics were painted animals and birds, as one may see in the obelisks which were brought to this city from Egypt. And if I would speak of poetry, it seems to me not difficult to show how true a sister she is of painting. But that Signor Francisco may know how much he stands in need of poetry and how much he may learn from the best poetry, I wish to show him (although the subject is better suited to a younger man) how greatly the poets care for his art and profession and exalt it and praise it when finished and perfect. And it would seem indeed that the whole aim of the poets has been to teach the excellence of painting, and that with such softness and music in their verse, such force and wealth of language, that I know not how you can repay them, since one of the things on which they bestow most care and labour (I speak of celebrated poets) is to paint well and imitate good painting. And this is the excellence which they wish most immediately and carefully to express in their work, and he who can attain this is considered the best and most famous poet. Let me remind you that the prince of them, Virgil, falls asleep at the foot of a beech and paints in words the shape of two jars wrought by Alcymedon and a grotto overgrown with a wild vine, and goats chewing the sallows, and blue hills smoking in the distance. And there he lies head on hand the livelong day, to see what winds and clouds he shall paint when he makes Aeolus rage, and how he shall paint the harbour of Carthage, with its bay surrounded by hills and woods, and an adjacent island. Then he paints Troy burning, and later the festivities in Sicily; and near Cumae the road to Hell, with many monsters and chimeras and many souls passing over Acheron; and then the Elysian fields, the communing of the blest and the punishment and torments of the impious; then the arms of Vulcan, excellently painted; and presently an amazon and the fierce bareheaded Turnus. He paints the rout of battle, many deaths, the fate of many famous men and many spoils and triumphs. You may read all Virgil and find in him nothing but the art of a Michael Angelo!

Lucan fills a hundred pages in painting an enchantress and the fair commencement of a battle; Ovid is but one continuous painting; Statius paints the house of Sleep and the walls of mighty Thebes. The poet Lucretius likewise paints, as do Tibullus and Catullus and Propertius. Another paints a spring and a wood near it and Pan as a shepherd playing on his lyre among the sheep; another paints a shrine and nymphs round it dancing; another draws a drunken Bacchus surrounded by frenzied women, with Silenus half falling from his ass and only held on by the help of a stalwart satyr, who carries a wine-skin. Even the satiric poets paint the picture of the labyrinth. And what of the lyric poets, and the epigrammatic Martial and the tragic and comic poets; is not theirs deliberate painting? And it is not merely I who say so: each of them admits that he is painting and calls painting dumb poetry.

Here I said: Signor Lattanzio, that they should call painting dumb poetry only implies, I think, that they were unskilled in painting, for had they realized how much more she speaks and sets forth than her sister they would not have said it; and I will rather maintain that poetry is the dumb art.

How will you prove that, O Spaniard, said the Signora Marchesa, and make it good that painting is not dumb and that poetry is? Let us have your arguments, since in no other discussion could we better employ this day and it may be long ere the present company meet elsewhere.

How, I answered, can your Excellency wish me to occupy your time with my scant learning, especially when I am the disciple of a dumb and voiceless lady and, moreover, it is growing late, if the light in those windows deceive me not? And how would you have me praise my love before her husband and in so honourable a company of those who appreciate her worth? For if I had to deal with obstinate enemies, perhaps I might do so; and yet I am wrong, for it were easier to overcome any such enemies than to content her friends. But if your noble Excellency is so desirous to see how little I can speak, I will speak not as an enemy of poetry, to which I am grateful and greatly indebted in the practice of my high profession and in my ambition to attain perfection in it, but to defend that other lady who is even more mine and to serve whom only I delight to be alive, by whose power I have a voice and speak, albeit she is dumb, merely from having once chanced to see her move her eyes. And if she can teach to speak with her eyes, what would she not do if I were to see her open her wise lips? Good poets, as Signor Lattanzio said, do no more than say in words what even mediocre painters actually create; for the former relate what the latter express and produce. Poets with lengthy disquisitions do not always arrest the ear; painters satisfy the eye and charm and enchant all men as with some lovely spectacle. And good poets are chiefly concerned with this, and consider it the height of their art, in words (and perhaps at excessive length) to show you a storm at sea or a burning city as if it were painted, and if they could they would have painted it; and when you have been at pains to read the whole account of the storm you have already forgotten the beginning and have present to your mind the one short verse actually before your eyes. How much more eloquent is painting, which shows you at one moment that storm with its thunder and lightning, the waves and shattered ships and the rocks, and you see

*Omniaque viris ostentant praesentem mortem,*

and in the same passage

*Extemplo Aeneas . . . tendens ad sidera palmas*

and

*Tres Eurus abreptas in saxa latentia torquet*
*Emissamque hyemem sensit Neptunus, et imis . . .*

And in the same way it presents very vividly all that burning of the city, set forth and seen in all its parts as though it were all actually true: here are men fleeing through the streets and squares; there they throw themselves down from the walls and towers; yonder stand temples half in ruins and the flames gleam on the surface of the river; the Sigean shores are lit up; Panthus limps away with the idols in his arms, holding his grandson by the hand; the Trojan horse gives birth to armed men in a great square; there Neptune in fury assails the walls, and Pyrrhus beheads Priam; Aeneas goes, with his father on his back, and Ascanius and Creusa follow him full of fear through the dark night; and all this so vividly and naturally, in its entirety, that often you are driven to imagine that you are not safe and are glad to know that it is but a picture, without fell power to do you hurt. And it does not show this in scattered words, of which you can remember only the line immediately before your eyes, forgetting the past and ignorant of what is to come (and even this one line only the ears of a grammarian can interpret); but the eyes are visibly delighted as though the scene were true, and the ears seem to hear the very cries and shouts of these painted figures. You seem to smell the smoke and shun the flame, to go in fear of the crumbling ruins; you pause to lend a hand to those who fall, to assist those who are fighting against odds, you flee with those who flee, and join a group of those who are making a stand. And it satisfies not only the discreet but the simple, peasants and old women; and further,

Sarmatians and Indians and Persians (who never understood the poetry of Virgil or Homer, dumb indeed to them) will delight in and understand this work with great ease and pleasure; and the barbarian then ceases to be a barbarian and by means of painting's eloquence understands what no other poetry nor versification could teach him. For the laws of painting say: In ipsa legunt qui litteras nesciunt, and farther on: Pro lectione pictura est. When Cebes the Theban wished to write down a moral on human life, he fashioned and painted it on a panel, holding that he would so best express it, and that it would be nobler so and more easily understood of men; and in order to speak he wished to know rather how to paint than how to write. But if even so poetry assert that a painted Venus at the feet of Jupiter does not speak, nor Turnus, showing his courage before King Latinus, not even this argument will render the learned art of painting dumb nor prevent her from speaking and from proving that in this as in all else she is first, or at least walks abreast of the Lady Poetry. For a great painter will paint Venus weeping at the feet of Jupiter with these advantages over the poet; first, he paints the sky where this occurs and the person and dress and action or movement of Jupiter and of his eagle and his thunderbolt; and he will paint fully the extravagant beauty of Venus and the light folds of her robe and all her suppliant figure, so lightly and with such delicate skill that, although her lips do not speak, yet her eyes and mouth and hands appear really to be speaking (for when a harsh-voiced pedagogue reads out the words and sayings of Venus it is not her soft sweet accents that you hear) and seem to utter those pitiful complaints which Virgilius Maro attributes to her. And in the same way the painter will give a fuller presentation of King Latinus and a clear picture of the council of the Laurentes, some with troubled face, others more constant and quiet, different in dress and look and features, in age and movements; all of which a poet cannot render without becoming excessively confused and prolix. But the painter will do it, and increase the pleasure and emotion caused by his picture. In the same way he will set before your eyes the spirited image of Turnus, so fierce and boastful against coward Drances that you seem to grow afraid of him as you hear him say:

*Larga quidem semper, Drance, tibi copia fandi.*

Hence I, with my meagre understanding, the disciple of a voiceless mistress, hold that painting has even greater power than poetry to produce higher effects and forcibly and vehemently move the mind and soul to gaiety and laughter or to sadness and tears, and that its eloquence is more effective. But let the Muse Calliope be judge in this dispute. I shall be glad to abide by her decision.

With that I ended; but the Signora Marchesa deigned thus to flatter me: You, Messer Francisco, have acquitted yourself so well on behalf of Painting, your love, that if Messer Michael fails to show a like affection for her we shall perhaps have to divorce her from him and send her away with you to Portugal.

And Michael smiling said: It is because he knows, Signora, that I am divorced from her already and have given her to him, having no longer strength for so great a passion, that he has spoken of her as his very own.

I admit, Signora, I said, that he has given her to me, but she refuses to go with me and still abides with him; and, whatever my own worth, I would not wish to see her in my country yet, since few there know how to esteem her, and even the most serene king would not favour her, except in rare moments of leisure, especially when engaged with thoughts of war, where she has no place; and she would grow weary, and perhaps in her annoyance throw herself one day into the sea, which is hard by, and make me often repeat those verses:

*Audieras, et fama fuit; sed opera tantum*
*Nostra valent, Lycida, tela inter martia quantum*
*Chaonias dicunt aquila veniente columbas.*[1]

But if she were of use in time of war I would welcome her indeed.

I see what you are aiming at, said the Signora Marchesa; but since the day is far spent, let your inquiry stand over for next Sunday. And with these words she rose, and we rose with her, and went away. (*Second Dialogue*)

SIGNOR Michael indeed, I answered, is under an obligation to fulfil the intention of the Signora Marchesa when in our last conversation she understood my meaning and all but promised to show me whether the most precious art of painting be wholly useless in wartime, for I remember that it was with this intent that her Excellency summoned us for last Sunday, when we failed to meet.

Michael then laughed and said: So, Master Francisco, you would have the Signora Marchesa's power to be as great in her absence as in her presence? Well, since you have such faith in her, I would not willingly make you lose it.

All were of the same mind, and forthwith Michael Angelo began to speak:

What can be more serviceable in the business and enterprise of war than the art of painting, or what more useful in the stress of sieges and assaults? Know you not that when Pope Clement and the Spaniards were besieging Florence it was only by the work and skill of the painter Michael Angelo that the besieged were long defended, if not the city actually delivered? And the besieging captains and soldiers were for long overwhelmed and harassed and slain by the defences and supports that I set up on the towers, lining them in a night with sacks of wool, and excavating others and filling them with fine powder, with which I heated the Spaniards' blood and hoisted them in fragments into the air. So that I consider great painting not only useful but indispensable in wartime, for the machines and instruments of war, for catapults, battering-rams, mantlets, 'tortoises', and iron-clad towers and bridges, and (since this evil iron age no longer uses these weapons but rejects them) for the fashioning of mortars, guns, strong cannon, and muskets; and especially for the shape and proportions of all forts and rocks, bastions, moats, mines, countermines, trenches, parapets, casemates; for ramparts and escarpments, ravelins, gabions, embrasures, battlements; for the fashioning of bridges and scaling-ladders, for besieging camps and dressing the files of soldiers and ordering squadrons; for the cunning design of arms and the emblems of banners and standards and the devices for shields and helmets; and also for the new coats of arms and crests and scutcheons which are bestowed on those who acquit themselves well on the field of battle; for the painting of caparisons (instructing, that is, lesser painters how they should be painted, although in the case of renowned princes great painters may paint the caparisons of their horses and their bucklers and even their tents); for the right ordering and selection in everything, and for the proper pattern and matching of colours and liveries, in which few have skill. Besides all this, drawing is of greatest use in war in making plans of distant places and the shape of mountain ranges and their passes and of bays and sea-ports; the shape of cities and fortresses, small and great, their walls and the form and position of their gates; and to show the roads and rivers and sea-shores, the lakes and marshes which must be avoided or crossed; the direction and length of deserts and sandy spaces on bad roads, and of woods and forests; otherwise all this will be vague, whereas in these plans and drawings it will be very plain and intelligible; all of which is of great importance in warlike enterprises, so that the painter's drawings greatly assist and concern the plans and designs of the general. And is it not excellent for a brave officer to be able to show to his raw recruits the plan of the city they are about to assault, or the river which they must cross to-morrow, the mountains and towns? The Italians, at least, say that if the Emperor, when he attacked Provence, had ordered a drawing to be made of the course of the river Rhone, he would not have met with losses so severe nor retired with his army so disarrayed nor would they in Rome have drawn him as a crab moving sideways, which kept going back instead of forwards, with the legend of the pillars of Hercules: 'Plus ultra'. And I am persuaded that Alexander the Great in his high enterprises would often consult the genius of Apelles, if he could not himself draw. And in the deeds done and the commentaries written by the monarch Julius Caesar we may judge how greatly he profited by the art of drawing, through some excellent draughtsman in his army. I even hold that Caesar himself had great understanding of the art of painting, since the great captain Pompey drew in excellent style, yet was vanquished by Caesar as the better draughtsman. I assert in fact that the modern general of a great army who has not skill and understanding of the art of painting and is unable to draw will be incapable of great prowess and warlike deeds; while he who understands and esteems it will win great glory and renown, and will know where he is and where he is going and the lines of attack and retreat; and will enhance his victory, not without reason, since painting in war is not only useful but indispensable. And what country under the sun is there more warlike than our Italy, or where there are more continual wars and great routs and fiercely pressed sieges? And what country is there under the sun where painting is more esteemed and prized?

Michael Angelo here paused for breath, and Zapata began:

It seems to me, Messer Michael, that in arming so splendidly Francisco de Hollanda's lady you have disarmed the Emperor Charles, forgetting that in this company the Colonnas outnumber the Orsini. My revenge shall consist in begging you, since you have shown the worth of painting in war, that you should now say what it is able to do in time of peace, for you have said so much of its usefulness in war that I do not think you will find so much to say in its praise as a civilian.

Then he laughed and answered:

Your Worship must not consider me an Orsini; with the memory of a Colonna so fresh in our minds, I am certainly one of the columns between which the crab moved.

And presently he continued: But if it cost me some trouble to set forth the usefulness of this art in wartime, I hope it will be much less difficult to show its worth in the tranquil civilian days of peace; for in such times princes are wont to set their pleasure and expense on things of slight importance and even of no worth at all; and in this idleness we see men cunning enough to gain for themselves a name without any skill out of obscure and worthless things, winning profit and riches for themselves and leaving the losses to those from whom they extract the profit. In independent states and senates, under a senate and republic, painting is employed largely for public purposes, to wit, in cathedrals and temples, courts of justice, tribunals, porticoes, basilicas and palaces, and in libraries and in other public places and general ornaments; and in the same way every noble citizen owns in private a goodly part of painting in their palaces and chapels, their country houses and vineyards. And if in states where no one is permitted to exalt himself above his neighbours painters receive commissions which make them rich and wealthy, how much more in loyal and peaceful kingdoms where God has put it in the power of a single person to carry out all the magnificent expenditure and sumptuous works which his pleasure and honour may desire and demand, how much more should use be made of this useful art and science; more especially as painting is so generous an art that a painter can by himself without any help do many things which many men together could not do, and a prince would be his own worst enemy (quite apart from the injury done to the noble arts) if, as soon as he can attain quiet and holy peace, he does not undertake great works of painting, both for the embellishment and glory of his state and for his private enjoyment and the recreation of his spirit. And since painting serves for so many things in time of peace, it would almost seem that the main object of attaining peace after such toil of arms is that painting should have leisure to produce its works and effects in the quiet which they deserve and need, after the great services rendered by it in war. And indeed what will remain of a great victory or an heroic deed if, on the return of peace, it does not leave, through painting and architecture, an everlasting memory, a thing so great and necessary among men, in arches and trophies and tombs and many other constructions? And Augustus Caesar, when, all the world at peace, he closed the doors of the Temple of Janus, was surely of my opinion, since, after closing the doors of iron, he opened those of gold and spent the imperial treasure more lavishly in peace than he had in war; and it may be, in those mighty and magnificent works with which he adorned the Mount Palatine and the Forum, that he gave for a single painted figure as much as a month's pay for a company of soldiers. Thus peace must be desired by great princes in order to enrich their states with great works of art, for the adornment of their dignity and fame, and for their own spiritual pleasure in the delight of their eyes.

I know not, Signor Michael, said I, how you will prove to me that Augustus may have paid for one painted figure as much as a company of soldiers would cost him in a month; were you to say that in Spain, perhaps they would find it harder to believe than that there could be in Italy painters execrable enough to paint the Emperor with the legs of a crab and the legend 'Plus ultra'.

Then for the second time, although the Marchesa was absent, Signor Michael laughed; and he said:

I know that in Spain they pay less well for painting than they do in Italy, and being accustomed to smaller rewards you will marvel at the large sums given; I know about it from a Portuguese servant I had; but that is why painters live here, that is why there are painters here and not in the Spains. And in this the Spaniards are of the strangest nobility! For you will find them ready enough to go into ecstasies in their praise of and delight in painting; but press them further and they have not the spirit to order or pay for the slightest work; and, what I consider viler still, they are amazed if you tell them of the great sums given in Italy for works of painting, for they do not seem to me in this to act up to their boasted nobility, if only that they should not turn round and disdain that which, before they were brought down to hard facts, they exalted to the skies, since in so doing they discredit themselves and disgrace their vaunted nobility, not to mention the art which will always be honoured so long as there are men and a city in Italy. That is why a painter should not wish to live elsewhere than in this country. And you, Messer Francisco de Hollanda, if you think to thrive by the art of painting in Spain or Portugal, I tell you now that you nourish a vain and empty hope, and I would advise you rather to live in France or Italy, where genius is recognized and great painting held in high esteem. For there are to be found private gentlemen here who do not greatly care for painting, such as Andrea Doria, who nevertheless painted his palace magnificently and munificently rewarded the master Perino, his painter; or like the Cardinal Farnese, who does not know what painting is and yet gave the same Perino a very fair salary, simply that he should be called his painter; twenty crusados a month and rations for the support of himself and a horse and servant, besides paying generously for his works. You may judge what a Cardinal della Valle or a Cardinal di Cesi would do! And in the same way Pope Paul, although he is not very artistic nor versed in painting, treats me generously, or at least gives me much more than I ever asked. And here is Urbino, my servant, to whom, merely to mix my colours, he gives ten crusados a month, besides rations in the palace. I say nothing of his idle favours and flatteries, of which I am sometimes ashamed. And what shall I say of the fortunate Venetian Sebastiano who, albeit the times were not favorable, received from the Pope the Uffizio del Piombo, with the honour and profit that such a post entails, although the lazy man painted but two pictures in Rome, in neither of which Messer Francisco may have found anything very wonderful.

Thus in this country even those who do not greatly esteem painting give a better price for it than they who are loud in its praises in Spain and Portugal; so that I give you this advice, as to a son: not to leave Italy; for if you do, I fear you may regret it.

I thank you for your advice, Signor Michael Angelo, I said, yet I serve the King of Portugal; in Portugal I was born and hope to die and not in Italy. But since you show that there is so great a difference in valuing painting in Italy and in Spain, be so kind as to tell me how one should value painting, for I am so diffident in the matter that I do not trust myself to value any work of art.

What do you mean by valuing? he answered. Would you have the painting of which you and I speak valued in terms of money or that any one should be able so to value it? For, as for me, I value as of the highest price the work done by a great painter, even if he have spent little time over it; for if he has spent much, who is there who could tell its worth? And I value very little that which an unskilful painter has painted in many years of work, however much they call him a painter; for works are not to be judged by the amount of useless labour spent on them but by the worth of the skill and mastery of their author; were it not so, they would not pay a larger sum to a lawyer for giving an hour's attention to an important case than to a weaver for all the cloth he weaves during his whole life or to a peasant who toils all day at his digging. 'E por tal variar natura è bella.'

But very foolish is the valuation made by one who does not understand what is good or bad in a work of art; and some which are worth little are valued high, while others of more worth are valued at a price which does not compensate for the care that has gone to their painting nor for the disgust of the painter when he knows how his work is to be valued and his extreme annoyance at having to ask to be paid by an inartistic treasurer. I do not think that the ancient painters were content with these Spanish prices and valuations of yours; I am sure they were not, for we know that some of them were so liberal and magnificent that, knowing that there was not enough money in their country to pay for their works, they gave them liberally for nothing, after having spent on their work time and intellectual labour and money. Of these were Zeuxis of Heraclea and Polignotus of Thasos, and others. Others, more impatient, ruined and destroyed the works which they had made with so much pains and toil when they saw that they were not paid for as they deserved. There was, for instance, a painter who at the bidding of Caesar painted a panel and asked for it so large a sum of money that Caesar refused to give it (perhaps to test him); thereupon the painter seized the panel and was about to break it in pieces, with his wife and children round him lamenting so great a loss; but Caesar then threw over him a charm such as became a Caesar and paid him double what he had asked, telling him he was mad if he expected to outdo Caesar.

Pray, Signor Michael, said Zapata the Spaniard, explain a doubt of mine about the art of painting: why is it that artists sometimes, as we see in many parts of this city, paint a thousand monsters and animals, some of them with a woman's face and the lower parts and tail of a fish, others with the arms of tigers and with wings, or with a man's face; anything in fact that delights the painter's fancy and has never existed.

I shall be glad, said Michael, to tell you why it is the custom to paint things that have never existed and how reasonable is this licence and how it accords with the truth; for some critics, not understanding the matter, are wont to say that Horace, the lyric poet, wrote those lines in dispraise of painters:

> *Pictoribus atque poetis*
> *Quidlibet audendi semper fuit aequa potestas:*
> *Scimus, et hanc veniam petimusque damusque vicissim.*

And in this sentence he does in nowise blame painters but praises and favours them, since he says that poets and painters have licence to dare, that is to dare what they choose. And this insight and power they have always had; for whenever (as very rarely happens) a great painter makes a work which seems to be artificial and false, this falseness is truth; and greater truth in that place would be a lie. For he will not paint anything that cannot exist according to its nature; he will not paint a man's hand with ten fingers, nor paint a horse with the ears of a bull or a camel's hump; nor will he paint the foot of an elephant with the same feeling as the foot of a horse, nor the arm or face of a child like those of an old man; nor an ear or eye even half an inch out of its proper place; not even the hidden vein of an arm may he place where he will; for all such things are most false. But if, in order to observe what is proper to a time and place, he exchange the parts or limbs (as in grotesque work which would otherwise be very false and insipid) and convert a griffin or a deer downwards into a dolphin or upwards into any shape he may choose, putting wings in place of arms, and cutting away the arms if wings are more suitable, this converted limb, of lion or horse or bird, will be most perfect according to its nature; and this may seem false but can really only be called ingenious or monstrous. And sometimes it is more in accordance with reason to paint a monstrosity (to vary and relax the senses and the object presented to men's eyes, since sometimes they desire to see what they have never seen and think cannot exist) rather than the ordinary figure, admirable though it be, of man or animals. And this insatiable desire of man sometimes prefers to an ordinary building, with its pillars and windows and doors, one falsely constructed in grotesque style, with pillars formed of children growing out of the stalks of flowers, with architraves and cornices of branches of myrtle and doorways of reeds and other things, all seeming impossible and contrary to reason; yet, it may be really great work if it is made by a skilful artist.

And when he ceased, I said: Do you not think, Sir, that this false work is much more suitable in its place, as for instance in a country residence or pleasure-house, than would be something in itself very natural, as a procession of monks or King David doing penance, which it is quite out of place to set elsewhere than in a chapel? And do you not think that for the painting of a garden or fountain it is more fitting to have the god Pan playing his lyre or a woman with the tail of a fish or with wings, although it be a thing rarely seen? And that it is much more false to set correct things out of their place than to invent an imaginary one in a place that fits it? It is from this reasoning that all the other so-called impossibilities of painting proceed. And if any be unconvinced and say 'How is it possible that a woman with a beautiful face should have the tail of a fish or the feet of a swift deer or ounce or wings on her sides like an angel?' one might answer that, if that anomaly be rightly proportioned in each of its parts, then it is normal and very natural; and that a painter is worthy of great praise if he paint an impossible thing which has never been seen with such art and skill that it seems alive and possible and causes men to wish that such things did actually exist and to say that one might pull feathers out of those wings and that it is moving its hands and eyes. And thus, if a man, as a certain book records, paint a hare such that it requires a legend under it to distinguish it from the pursuing hound, he may be said to have painted a thing extremely false, which it would be harder to discover among the perfect works of Nature than a beautiful woman with wings or the tail of a fish.

They argeed with what I said; even Zapata, who was not greatly versed in the excellences of painting. And seeing that the conversation was not lost upon us, the master, Michael Angelo, said: And what a noble thing is a true propriety in painting! How little painters who are not painters trouble to observe it, and how watchfully the great painter studies it!

Are there painters who are not painters? asked Zapata.

Many enough, answered the painter; but as the undiscerning common people always likes what it ought to detest and blames that which is most deserving of praise, it is not astonishing that so many mistakes should be made about painting, an art worthy only of lofty intellects; for, without judgement or reason or any skill in distinguishing, they give the name of painter alike to a man who has no art beyond his oils and thick or fine paintbrushes, and to the illustrious painter who is born once in many years (which I consider a very great thing). And as there are painters who are not painters, so there is painting which is not painting, the work of the same. And the marvellous thing is that the bad painter is unable to conceive the image or desire of good painting in his mind, for the work of his hands usually answers pretty well to the thought in his mind, or is but little worse; for if his imagination could conceive good or masterly painting, his hand could not be so abject as not to reproduce some part or trace of his noble aspiration. But high aspiration in this science belongs only to the mind which understands what is good and how much thereof it is able to attain. And the extreme difference between the aspirations of a high and of a low understanding in painting is indeed a tremendous thing.

Here Messer Lattanzio, who had for some time been silent, said:

One thing I cannot forgive bad painters, and that is their lack of taste in painting images without devotion or judgement in the churches. And I should like our discussion to end with this subject. And certainly no one can approve the want of care with which a very unskilful painter (to call him a painter) sets himself to paint holy images so rashly and ignorantly that, instead of moving men to tears and devotion, they sometimes rather provoke to laughter.

Indeed this is so high an undertaking, went on Michael Angelo, that in order to imitate in some degree the venerable image of Our Lord, it is not enough to be a painter, a great and skilful master; I believe that he must further be of blameless life, even if possible a saint, that the Holy Spirit may inspire his understanding. We read that Alexander the Great forbade on pain of a heavy penalty any other painter to paint him except Apelles, considering him alone capable of painting him with that severity of aspect and liberal look which could not be seen by the Greeks without being praised nor by the barbarians without being feared and worshipped. And if a poor man of this earth made this edict about his portraits, how much more should princes of the Church or State most carefully enact that no one should paint the loving-kindness and mercy of Our Redeemer nor the purity of Our Lady and of the saints except the most eminent painters they can find in their kingdoms and domains. Such a decree would bring fame and praise to any ruler. And in the Old Testament it was the will of God the Father that those who had merely to adorn and paint the art of the covenant should not only be great and eminent masters but should be inspired with His grace and wisdom; for God said unto Moses that He would fill them with the wisdom and understanding of His spirit in order that they might be able to devise and do all that it could devise and do. And if it was the will of God the Father that the ark of His law should be skilfully adorned and painted, how much more must it be His will that care and judgement should be bestowed on copying His serene countenance and that of His Son our Lord, and the tranquillity, chastity, and beauty of the glorious Virgin Mary, copied by St. Luke the Evangelist; and likewise in the Holy of Holies the countenance of the Saviour which is in San Giovanni Laterano, as we all know, and Messer Francisco better than any. For often badly wrought images distract the attention and prevent devotion, at least with persons who have but little; while those which are divinely fashioned excite even those who have little devotion or sensibility to contemplation and tears and by their austere beauty inspire them with great reverence and fear.

HOW is it possible, replied Messer Lattanzio, that one who has never painted in oil should be able to paint in oil, or that one who has only painted in miniature should be able to paint large figures?

And as I did not answer, Michael Angelo answered for me:

Your Worship need not be astonished, and I will here make a statement concerning the noble art of painting. Let this be plain to all: design, or as it is called by another name, drawing, constitutes the fountain-head and substance of painting and sculpture and architecture and every other kind of painting and is the root of all sciences. Let him who has attained the possession of this be assured that he possesses a great treasure; he will be able to make figures taller than any tower, both painted and as statues, and he will find no wall or side of a building that will not prove narrow and small for his great imaginings. He will be able to paint frescoes in the old Italian fashion, with all its usual mingling and variety of colours; he will be able to paint very smoothly in oil, with more skill, daring, and patience than mere painters can; finally, in the scanty space of a piece of parchment he will prove himself a great and most perfect artist, as great as in those other ways. And because the power of design or drawing is great, so very great, Messer Francisco de Hollanda can, if he choose, paint whatsoever he can draw.

I will not make bold to question you as to another doubt I have, said Messer Lattanzio.

Your Worship may make bold, said Michael Angelo; for since we have sacrificed the day to painting, let us offer it also a part of the night which is coming on.

Well, I wish to know in sum what is the subject of this so rare and exquisite art of painting? What is it? Must it paint jousts and battles? Kings and emperors adorned with brocade, and finely attired maidens? Or landscapes, fields, and cities? Or perhaps the subject of painting should be an angel or some saint? Or the shape of this earth of ours? What should it be? And should it be done in gold or in silver, with delicate tints or in brighter colours?

Painting, Michael Angelo began to explain, is not so great a thing as any of those you have mentioned; painting, which I so greatly honour and praise, is merely to copy with great care and skill one single thing of those made by immortal God, invented and painted by Him, in His own image and the lower creation, animals and birds, perfect each according to its kind. And in my opinion that painting is excellent and divine which most resembles and best copies any work of immortal God, whether it be a human figure or a wild and strange beast or a simple straightforward fish or a bird of the sky or any other creature; and that not in gold or silver or delicate tints but simply drawn with a brush or with chalk or with a pencil in black and white. To copy each one of those things after its kind seems to me to be indeed to imitate the work of God; but that work of painting will be most noble and excellent which copies the noblest object and does so with most delicacy and skill. And who is so barbarous as not to understand that the foot of a man is nobler than his shoe, and his skin nobler than that of the sheep with which he is clothed, and not to be able to estimate the worth and degree of each thing accordingly? Yet I do not say that, because a cat or a wolf is a common thing, he who paints them skilfully will not have as much merit as he who paints a horse or the body of a lion; for, as I have already said, the simple form of a fish has the same excellence and beauty of proportion as the figure of a man, and indeed as that of the whole world with its cities. But one must give each thing its own degree of importance according to the labour and study that one thing demands more than another, and thus disabuse certain ignorant critics who said that some painters painted faces well but could not paint the rest adequately. Others said that in Flanders they painted clothes and trees extremely well, and some affirmed that in Italy they excelled in the nude and in symmetry and proportion; and they make other criticisms of the same kind. But in my opinion the man who can merely make and draw well a foot or a hand or a neck will be able to paint all created things; and there are painters who paint everywhere in the world with so little excellence and perfection that it were better not to paint them at all. And the skill of a great painter is shown in the fear with which he paints a thing in proportion as he understands it, and in the same way the ignorance of others appears in the presumptuous boldness with which they lavish their unskilful art. And a man may be an excellent painter who has never painted more than a single figure and even so deserves more honour and renown than those who have painted a thousand pictures; and he is better skilled in what he does not do than they in what they do. And not only is this so but what may seem a greater miracle is that a good painter, making a beginning with a simple outline, will at once be recognized as an Apelles, if he is one; if he is an ignorant painter he will be recognized as such. There is no need of more, no more time nor proof nor examination in the eyes of those who understand the matter and know that by a single straight line Apelles could be distinguished from that other imortal Greek painter, Protogenes.

Here Michael Angelo was silent, and I went on: It is also a strange thing that an excellent master cannot, even if he wish and attempt to do it, so change and vitiate his hand as to do anything that will seem to be the work of an apprentice; for any one who examines the work carefully will discover in it some indication that it is the work of a skilful hand. On the other hand, the unskilful, however much he strive to do the slightest thing which will appear to be the work of a great man, will waste his pains, for it will be known at once as not the work of the great man but of an apprentice. But I would now know this of Signor Michael Angelo, to see if he agrees with my opinion: I would have him tell me whether it is better to work quickly or slowly.

He answered: I will tell you; to do anything with great facility and skill is useful and good, and it is a gift of immortal God that a man should be able to paint in a few hours what another must work at for many days; otherwise Pausias of Sicyon would not have striven so hard to make a perfect painting of a child in a single day. He therefore who, working quickly, paints as well as he who works slowly deserves the greater praise; but if in his hand's facility he overstep a certain limit which art may not licitly overstep, he ought rather to paint more slowly and with greater care; for a great and excellent painter has no right to allow himself to be deceived by delight in his quickness if it here and there cause him to forget and overlook the great task of perfection, which must be his continual aim. It is thus not a fault to be a little slow or even very slow and to spend much time and care on a work if the object be greater perfection; it is only lack of skill that is a defect. And I would tell you, Francisco de Hollanda, a very great excellence of this art of ours, an excellence which you perhaps already know of and will I think consider supreme: that what one must most toil and labour with hard work and study to attain in a work of painting is that, after much labour spent on it, it should seem to have been done almost rapidly and with no labour at all, although in fact it was not so. And this needs most excellent skill and art. Sometimes, but very rarely, such a result is obtained with little labour; the important thing is that it should seem done very easily, although it has cost hard work. Plutarch in a book entitled *De liberis educandis* relates that an indifferent painter showed Apelles what he was doing, with the words: 'This picture I have this moment done with my own hand'; and Apelles replied: 'Even had you not told me, I should have known that it was your work and done quickly, and I am astonished that you do not paint many such in a day.' But, if one must either fail or succeed, I had rather one should fail or succeed quickly than slowly, and that my painter should paint with spirit and a little less well than very laboriously and a little, but not much, better.

## *Letter to M. Benedetto Varchi*

I have received your little book, and will now endeavour to reply to your questions, though I fear it will be inefficiently. I should say that painting is considered to be more perfect in proportion as it approaches to the relief of sculpture, and that such relief becomes less effective in proportion as it approaches to painting. I therefore have been used to regard sculpture as the light of painting, and that between the one and the other, there might be the sort of difference of relation that there is between the sun and the moon. But since I have read in your work the passage in which you say that, speaking philosophically, those things which have the same end are in fact the same, I have altered my opinion, and would say that, if greater judgment, difficulty, impediment, and labour do not imply greater dignity, then painting and sculpture are one and the same thing; and that if such be the case, no painter should esteem sculpture inferior to painting, nor a sculptor in a similar way underrate painting. I understand by sculpture that which produces its effect by removing from the material used, be it what it may, the superfluous, and by painting, the laying on what is necessary to produce the desired effect.

Since, then, the same species of intelligence presides over both sculpture and painting, why not make peace between them, and close those endless disputes, the time consumed in which would be much better employed in producing works of art. If he who maintains that painting is more noble than sculpture, writes upon other subjects as he does upon this, my old woman would have written much better. Endless things might be stated much in the same manner, upon similar sciences; but they would consume, as I have already said, a great deal of time; and I have little to spare, for I am not only aged, but already, as it were, numbered with the dead. Therefore I am sure you will excuse me, and accept by best thanks for the great honour you have done me, which I little merit.

M.A.B.

## PAOLO UCCELLO

PAOLO DI DONO *(1397–1475), called Paolo Uccello, is considered the father of perspective in the Florentine painting of the Quattrocento. His well-known "Battles" interest us today for another reason: they seem to manifest a very pronounced tendency toward abstraction of forms and a pictorial construction divorced from all naturalistic inclinations.*

OH, what a gracious thing is perspective! (Quoted by Vasari)

## ALBRECHT DÜRER

ALBRECHT DÜRER *(1471–1528), born in Nuremberg, is the author of a number of theoretical writings, not all of which have come down to us. Only three are available:* Underweysung der Messung mit dem Zirckel und Richtscheyt *(instruction on measuring with compass and square rule), a treatise on Euclidean geometry;* Etliche Underricht zu Befestigung der Stett, Schloss und Flecken *(some lessons on fortifying cities, castles, and villages), more an engineer's work than an artist's; and* Hierinnen sind begriffen fier Bücher von menschlicher Proportion *(four books on human proportions), which is a sequence of mathematical researches undertaken in the hope of establishing a canon of ideal human beauty.*

THE artist must receive a gift from God to do in a day a drawing better than one which another will do in the course of a year and with all the equipment imaginable.

IF we were to ask how we are to make a beautiful figure, some would give answer: According to human judgment (i.e. common taste). Others would not agree thereto, neither should I without a good reason. Who then will give us certainty in this matter?

FOR Art standeth firmly fixed in Nature, and whoso can rend her forth thence, he only possesseth her.

THE more closely thy work abideth by life in its form, so much the better will it appear; and this is true. Wherefore nevermore imagine that thou either canst or shalt make anything better than God hath given power to his creatures to do.

BUT Beauty is so put together in men and so uncertain is our judgment about it, that we may perhaps find two men both beautiful and fair to look upon, and yet neither resembleth the other, in measure or kind, in any single point or part; and so blind is our perception that we shall not understand whether of the two is the more beautiful, and if we give an opinion on the matter it lacketh certainty.

ART barely expresses the beauty of things. I do not say the excellent and perfect [beauty], but that known to us, and still surpassing the strength of our understanding and fleeing the skill of our hands. (*Fier Bücher von menschlicher Proportion*)

## TITIAN

TIZIANO VECELLIO *(c. 1477–1576), called Titian, born in Pieve di Cadore, is undoubtedly the most important of the Venetian painters. He gave unflagging attention to problems of coloring.*

. . . MAKE the foliage glow from behind. (Titian to Aurolio Luini, quoted by Giovanni Paolo Lomazzo)

## LODOVICO DOLCE

LODOVICO DOLCE *(1508–1568), born in Venice, was a prolific writer in all literary genres, though the consensus is that he excelled in none. In his* Aretin: A Dialogue of Painting, *nonetheless, he reports on a trend in Venetian Renaissance painting that we would do well to examine.*

WHEN a painter catches the tints and soft blends of light areas and the particular character of objects, he makes his paintings seem alive, and such that they lack nothing but breath. The main point with coloring is the struggle light has with shadow, for which an intermediary uniting the two contraries is provided; and this makes the figures appear round and more or less distant, according to need. The eye must always be attentive to tints, especially of flesh, and to blending. For many painters make skins look like porphyry, as much in color as in hardness. And the shadows, too gloomy most of the time, end in pure black. Many make flesh too white, many make it too red. As for me, I prefer a dusky color over a too-white shade. Let no one believe that strong coloring consists in choosing beautiful colors—beautiful red-purples, beautiful blues, beautiful greens—[for it consists rather] in using them in an appropriate manner. It seems to me that one should treat overly appealing colors and labored figures with a certain reserve; one must see in the whole something like an agreeable stability. Above all, one must flee the excessive application that ruins everything.

## GIORGIO VASARI

GIORGIO VASARI *(1511–1574), born in Arezzo, is the author of the very valuable* Delle Vite de' più eccellenti pittori, scultori, ed architettori *(on the lives of the best painters, sculptors, and architects), to which art historians owe so much. Vasari was a better biographer than theoretician.*

SOME reach greatness in art by application, others by study; this one by imitation, another by knowledge of the sciences.

. . . EVERY man should content himself with performing such works as he may reasonably be supposed to be capable of and equal to, by his inclination and the gifts bestowed on him by nature, without seeking to contend for that which she has not qualified him to attain and this let him do, that he may not uselessly spend his time, fatiguing himself vainly, nay, not infreqently, to his own injury as well as discredit.

LET us point out the deplorable error, too often committed, of putting a painting or sculpture in a place other than the one the artist had in mind when he executed his work.

I maintain that drawing, that creative and vivifying principle of painting and sculpture, possessed all its perfection at the beginning of things. When God had made the earth and embellished the heavens with luminous bodies, he crossed the clarity of the air with His intelligence, descended on the earth, and made man. Who would dare say that this model shaped by the hand of the Almighty does not constitute the perfect type of all the beauties that sculpture craves and of the delicacy and harmonious collision of lights and shadows that painting seeks?

THE fancy cannot fully realize her own intentions unless these be to a certain extent submitted to the corporal eye, which then aids her to form a correct judgment. The nude form also demands much study before it can be well understood, nor can this ever be done without drawing the same on paper; to be compelled always to have nude or draped figures before the eyes while painting, is no small restraint, but when the hand has been well practised on paper, a certain facility both in designing and painting is gradually obtained, practice in art supervenes, the manner and the judgment are alike perfected, and that laboured mode of execution mentioned above [the paintings of Giorgione] is no more perceived. Another advantage resulting from drawing on paper is the store of valuable ideas which gradually fill the mind, enabling the artist to represent natural objects from his own thoughts, without being compelled to hold them constantly before him, nor does he who can draw, need to labour to hide his want of design beneath the attractions of colouring.

## TINTORETTO

JACOPO ROBUSTI *(1518–1594), called Il Tintoretto, was born in Venice. Like Titian, he was a great master of color. In addition, he manifests an often daring sense of composition, with great lyric leaps symphonically orchestrated.*

DRAW, draw some more, draw always!

THE loveliest colors are black and white because they give relief to figures by means of light and shadow. (Quoted in Charles Blanc, *Histoire des Peintres*)

# GIOVANNI PAOLO LOMAZZO

GIOVANNI PAOLO LOMAZZO *(1538–1600), wrote a* Treatise on the Art of Painting *(1584) that was highly successful immediately on publication. Considered a "mannerist," Lomazzo voiced opinions that nevertheless surpassed mannerism. He was in favor of painting that aimed at elaborating forms independently of their relations with objects. He also considered that the painter has the duty to express the psychological content of a subject.*

AND because in this place there falleth out a certaine precept of *Michael Angelo* much for our purpose, I will not conceale it, leaving the farther interpretation and understanding thereof to the iudicious reader. It is reported that *Michael Angelo* upon a time gave this observation to the Painter *Marcus de Sciena* his scholler; *that he should alwaies make a figure Pyramidall, Serpentlike, and multiplied by one two and three.* In which precept (in mine opinion) the whole mysterie of the arte consisteth. For the greatest grace and life that a picture can have is, that it expresses *Motion:* which the Painters call the Spirit of a picture: Nowe there is no forme so fitte to expresse this *motion,* as that of the flame of fire. Which according to *Aristotle* and the other Philosophers, is an elemente most active of all others: because the forme of the flame thereof is most apt for motion: for it hath a *Conus* or sharpe pointe wherewith it seeemeth [*sic*] to divide the aire, that so it may ascende to his proper sphere. So that a picture having this forme will bee most beautifull.

WHENCE wee see, that if the *Lights* bee well and proportionably bestowed throughout a body, which is yll proportioned and without muscles, it contenteth the eie of the beholder somewhat the more, by mooving him to a desire of seeing the muscles and other necessary partes, in such a body. . . . So that wee finde many painters, who being ignorant of the arte of proportions, onely by a little practize, in disposing their lights in some tolerable sorte, have notwithstanding bin reputed good workmen.

Because all colours have different qualities, therefore they cause diverse effects in the beholders, which arise from an inwarde contrariety of their causes. . . . Hence we may learne, the reason why some *colours* agree togither, and others doe not.

. . . [ONE MUST] never put two glowing colors side by side, but a color more or less muted beside another which is brighter, in such a way that the ones give value to the others, which observation whoever wants to be a painter can understand adequately from works like those of Antonio Allegri da Correggio. (*Traité de l'Art de la Peinture,* tr. Henri Guerlin, in *L'Art enseigné par les Maîtres*)

NOT constant fatigue, nor long studies, nor mental penetration, nor a solid foundation in letters, nor theological science, nor the help of astrology, nor geometric figures, nor knowledge of perspective, nor the harmonies of music, nor arithmetical proportions, nor three-dimensional models, nor historical recollections, nor poetic fictions, nor anatomical examples, nor expressions of feeling, and finally no philosophic knowledge or demonstrations can ever give someone who is not born to be a painter, that is, who has not carried natural inventiveness and grace with him from the cradle and swaddling clothes, the power to achieve any degree of excellence in that art. (*The Idea of the Temple of Painting*)

TO the end therefore that we may effectually raise and heighten all our pictures, we must be orderly guided by the direction of one principal light, greater then [*sic*] the rest, which must afterwardes also be diminished according to the distance, still observing this rule, as those famous painters did (*Leo: Vincent, Ra: Urbine, Gaudentius,* and *Cæsar Sestius*) ; who were therefore reputed worthy painters, because they used their light very sparingly, distributing them through out their pictures like precious stones.

# *Notes and Bibliography*

# NOTES

*The editors have chosen among the many scholarly notes to these selections those that have the greatest interest for the ordinary reader. Unless otherwise designated, these footnotes are taken from the edition of the book which appears in the Bibliography, but they are not numbered according to the original work.*

## FOREWORD

*1.* [The Foreword introduces all three volumes of THE ART OF PAINTING. *The Art of Painting from the Baroque through Postimpressionism* and *The Art of Painting in the Twentieth Century* follow this book in order of publication.—Ed.]

*2.* We must also explain the omission in whole or part of some very rigorous works, like Piero della Francesca's *De prospective pingendi,* Luca Pacioli's *De divina proportione,* and Albrecht Dürer's *Fier Bucher von menschlicher Proportion.* It would be difficult to draw self-contained quotations or excerpts from these works, which were mostly conceived as treatises on mathematical and geometric theorems, and including them in their entirety would have taken too much space. Further, they would have gone beyond the scope of our subject by giving this book a technical cast it does not pretend to have. We feel as well that the majority of such treatises seem to be either chess games or speculations on craft that give a less clear account of the *spirit* of painting than do simpler and more literary writings.

*3.* St. Augustine, *Confessions,* bk. X, *XXXV,* 54.

## INTRODUCTION

*1.* [Lascaux, or modern-day Montignac, and Eyzies-de-Tayac are in the department of Dordogne, in central southwest France; Altamira is in northwest Spain.—Tr.]

## *Pliny the Elder*

*1.* [Lychnites (also called Lychneus—from *lychnos,* a lamp—or Lygdos) is a white, semitransparent marble quarried on the island of Paros in the Aegean Sea and exported from the sixth century B.C.—Tr.]

## *Vitruvius*

*1.* [A sort of racket or bat.—Tr.]

*2.* Vitruvius suggests that the incrustation style corresponds to the tragic scenery; the architectural, to comic; the third, the landscape style, to satiric.

THE MIDDLE AGES

## *Dionysius of Phourna-Agrapha*

*1.* In a review on works relating to Arab architecture, M. Reinaud, a member of the Institut de France, writes: "The Greeks used a word for mosaics that meant construction in small stones. Adopting this type of decoration, the Arabs used the word *fsefysa,* which is an obvious translation of the Greek; their writers agree that this branch of the ornamental arts was of Christian origin. Thus, according to the Arab *Annals* of Eutychius the historian, when the Muslims invaded Palestine the first time, they found the Church of the Nativity in Bethlehem, which had been built at the direction of St. Helena, ornamented with *fsefysa.* And Ibn-Sa'id wrote that one of the conditions of the peace concluded at the beginning of the eighth century between Caliph Walid and the emperor of Constantinople was that the former would furnish a given quantity of *fsefysa* for the decoration of the mosque the Caliph was then having built at Damascus. Further, Al-Idrīsi, describing the mosque at Córdoba, wrote that the facing still to be seen on the walls of the Kibla was sent from Constantinople by the Emperor Romanus II to Caliph 'Abd-al-Raḥman (al Nāṣir) in the tenth century" (*"Notice sur deux ouvrages de M. Girault de Prangey," Journal asiatique,* no. 6 [1842], pp. 9–10).

We see the same word used in our manuscript to designate tesserae, but these were glass, transparent and bedded in gold, as the words indicate. In any event, these are the sort of tesserae that embellish the arches, the cupolas, the pendentives, and part of the interior walls of the Saint Sophias in Constantinople and Salonika,

Vatopédi and Laura monasteries on Mount Athos, Daphne near Athens, Saint Luke of Stiris monastery in Livadia, Greece, and the rotundas of Salonika and Ravenna. I brought back from the Salonika rotunda some of those little cubes of gilded glass, those little golden stones our manuscript refers to. It is interesting to note that mosaic work is Byzantine and Christian, and that the Arabs, whose architecture is borrowed, also borrowed even a large part of their ornamentation.

*2.* Oriental effusiveness and Byzantine luxuriance abound in the number and extremity of the epithet-laden qualifications.

*3.* [". . . Thou wicked and slothful servant! Knewest thou that I reap where I have not sown, and garner where I have not winnowed? Thou oughtest therefore to have put my money with the bankers, and I at my coming would have recovered what was mine with interest." (Luke 19: 22–23).—Tr.]

*4.* Panselinos was a twelfth-century painter—the Raphael, or better the Giotto, of the Byzantine school—whose frescoes may be seen in the main church in Karyes on Mount Athos. He is said to have lived in the time of Emperor Andronicus I. Noteworthy in design and expression, these frescoes have suffered much damage to their colors, which have darkened. It is hard to say that these paintings date surely from the twelfth century; but in fact they seemed to us much older than the similar paintings to be seen in the different Mount Athos and Meteora monasteries. Only Vatopédi and Laura on Mount Athos might have some as old.

*5.* In earlier times there must have been a great painting school at Salonika, which is the port of Mount Athos. The mosaics in the rotunda are the oldest and loveliest in all Greece; those in the small Saint Sophia, also in Salonika, are among the most remarkable. This city, where St. Paul left so many traces, today shows much decay. Master Panselinos and his disciple Dionysius would find only fragments of their paintings, and not even one poor artist who has really preserved their traditions.

[The Dionysius of this note is Dionysius of Phourna of Agrapha. In the appendix to M. Didron's *Christian Iconography,* it is stated that "The date of the original copy of this Byzantine guide is unknown. That which M. Didron found at Esphigmenon was held by the monks of Mount Athos to belong to the tenth or eleventh century, but was probably not older than the fifteenth or sixteenth. It is a copy of an older manuscript compiled by the monk Dionysius from the works of 'the celebrated and illustrous master Manuel Panselinos of Thessalonica,' a painter who, says Didron, 'was the Giotto of the Byzantine school,' and who flourished in the twelfth century, during the reign of the Emperor Adronicus the First. The copy of the manual of Dionysius first seen by Didron was in the hands of Joasaph, a monkish painter at Esphigmenon. The work, the date of which in its original form is unknown, had been extended and completed in successive centuries—but the copy in the hands of Joasaph was not three hundred years old. . . . A transcript of this guide is to be found in every atelier on Mount Athos."—Ed.]

*6.* Like the Latin rite, the Greek contains a great many different titles for the Virgin Mary. Our Lady of the Shoals, Our Lady of the Snows, Our Lady of Hope, our Lady of Good Help, and so on are used as invocations against avalanches, storms, despair, dangers of all kinds, etc. In Greece, the Virgin of Safe Conduct guides the faithful in all their undertakings, travelers on their trips, artists in their work. In the Athos monastery of Philotheu, an old painting on wood represents the Virgin holding Jesus, embracing the divine infant tenderly. Iconoclasts threw the painting into the sea, but it was found much later in a place from which a fresh-water spring still flows today. This Virgin is very revered, and is covered with pieces of gold.

*7.* The *Magnificat.*

*8.* [An anthem sung at matins.—Tr.]

*9.* The Transfiguration, so popular with Byzantine painters, is a most fitting subject for the artist, who transforms what he touches and changes the real into the idea. Greece thus enthroned art on Mount Tabor.

*10.* Abgar Ukkāmā, king of Edessa, had been very ill for a long time when he learned of the miracles Jesus was working. He therefore wrote to the Son of God to come and cure him, offering to divide his small city of Edessa with Jesus. Our Lord replied that he was shortly to accomplish his mission and could not come to the king, but that when he had returned to his Father he would send one of his disciples (this was the apostle Thaddeus), who would cure him. Disappointed at not seeing Jesus, Abgar wanted at least to have a picture of him, and therefore sent agents to the Son of God, charging them to have a painter do a portrait. "Jesus, to whom nothing is hidden and who can do all things," wrote John of Damascus, "took a piece of cloth, applied it to his face, and painted his own image on it. This image, perfectly preserved, is found today at Edessa" (John of Damascus, *Oratio prima de imaginibus,* vol. I of *Works;* Paris, 1712, folio, p. 320, also pp. 631, 632). See also Eusebius, *Historia ecclesiastica,* bk. I, chap. 3; and Nicephorus Callistus Xanthopoulos, *Historia ecclesiastica,* bk. II, chap. 7.

*11.* The Greeks so love images that they usually represent St. Luke in a studio painting the Virgin. With the French, St. Luke is almost always shown writing his Gospel, very rarely painting. This single fact suffices to characterize the two countries, at least with respect to art. The Greeks are painters; Western Europeans are sculptors and especially architects.

*12.* Before beginning to paint, Fra Angelico spent some time at prayer, thus practicing the pious advice given by the Byzantine painter.

*13.* That is, tracings.

*14. Sine manu facta,* on which the hand of man has not worked. These acheirous images are numerous, very old, and very precious. The best known are those of the Savior, of the Holy Face—the one imprinted on St. Veronica's napkin and the one Jesus had sent to King Abgar. There are pictures and statues of the Virgin which are similarly acheirous. These highly venerated works cannot be studied too carefully.

*15.* Father Macarios, the painter, who had me copy the *Guide,* complained to me that the painters on Mount Athos were working for money, and working as quickly as possible, no longer as in earlier times for sincerely pious reasons and with reflection.

*16.* Father Macarios, who has used these procedures, told me that his brushes were very poor. He was eager for me to send him some brushes from France, to which we were returning, because he knew they were excellent, he said.

*17.* The same painter, Father Macarios, regretted that the Mount Athos artists were forced to make everything themselves—their brushes, their glue, almost their very paints. He said, not incorrectly, that the considerable amount of time required for these preparations was to the detriment of the art, each painter doing these things badly and wasting a good deal of time at them. . . .

*18.* [Ampoli was a mixture of bole and ocher with a little soap and egg white. It was used to fix gold leaf.—Charpier & Seghers]

*19.* [Raki or rakiya is a mild alcoholic beverage made from plums in the Balkans, notably Serbia, and elsewhere.—Tr.]

*20.* It is unlikely that the author means the rouge used in cosmetics, a rather unstable color; it is rather a *white* used in painting, like ceruse (white lead), for example. . . . Moreover, didn't ceruse used to be called cosmetic white?—Paul Durand. . . .

*21.* [The quantities are missing. The quantities were left blank not only in this work but also in other Mount Athos manuscripts; such measures seem to have been left to the artists, whose experience would guide them. We are unsure of the measures, proportions, and meanings of the substances' names. The substances seem to have no modern-day equivalents, either because they are really different or because we have not found proper synonyms.—Charpier & Seghers]

*22.* [See footnote 21.—Tr.]

*23.* [Calacanthi seems to be a substance with a base derived from a spiny cactus.—Charpier & Seghers]

*24.* [See footnote 21.—Tr.]

*25.* I use the word *head* in translating because, as I say in a note below, the head is still the measure used for the proportions of the human body on Mount Athos. I have watched the painter Father Joasaph execute thirteen figures by working out and applying this calculation. . . .

*26.* Today on Mount Athos, painters no longer give their figures the height our manuscript prescribes. Instead of one on nine, it is only one on eight; the figures are shorter. They take the head as the unit of measure, and they say that the body should be eight heads tall. The pelvis is four heads from the heel and four heads from the top of the skull; it is exactly in the middle of the body. The knee is at five and a half heads. For the rest, as in the manuscript, from the root to the tip of the nose there is the same distance as from the root of the nose to the outer corner of an eye. Father Joasaph uses a compass to establish the proportions of his figures, the measure of the chest and all of the body. In our late Roman art, quite improperly called Byzantine, the figures measure nine heads; eight and a half in about the thirteenth century; eight to seven and a half in the fourteenth and fifteenth. In the sixteenth, with the Renaissance, the height increases, and some of Jean Goujon's figures reach nine heads in height. Le Sueur liked tall figures; if his St. Bruno praying on his knees were standing, he might be more than nine heads tall. The real measure of the human body is about seven and three-quarters or eight heads; this is the measure our painters and sculptors, who prefer reality to the ideal, have adopted in our times.

*27.* [Peseri was quite probably a drying oil. It was cooked in the sun, and when it reached the consistency of honey, it became an excellent glaze.—Charpier & Seghers]

*28.* Parisian artists might laugh at this economy recommended to the sacred artists, and yet one would do better to paint like Fathers Macarios and Joasaph than like certain of the very well-known artists in France.

*29.* [See footnote 21. Oxy was probably an acid.—Tr.]

*30.* It would perhaps be not without interest to sum up part of these instructions and procedures by putting down some observations I made and the interview I had with Father Joasaph, one of the best painters on Mount Athos. The procedures today are almost the same as in earlier times.

Here, then, is the method of fresco painting I saw used in the

Esphigmenu monastery on Mount Athos by Father Joasaph, his brother, a first-ranking student who was a deacon and who would inherit the atelier, and two young people twelve to fifteen years old.

The portico or narthex of the church, which was being painted when we passed through, had just been built; scaffolding had been put up for painting the frescoes at the top of the vault. In the courtyard, workers directed by the painters prepared the lime mixtures that would serve as plaster. Since two coats are laid on, there are two types of lime: the first, which looks like a sort of fine loam, is mixed with straw chopped fine, which gives it a yellowish color; cotton or flax is mixed with the second, which is smoother in quality. The yellow lime mixture is used for the first coat; it sticks to the wall better than the second. The second is of the white, smooth mixture, and because of the cotton makes a rather thick paste; this coat receives the painting.

The workmen handle the yellow lime, applying a layer about a half-centimeter thick to the wall. On that layer a skin of fine, white lime is spread a few hours later. This second process requires more care than the first, and I watched Father Joasaph's brother, also a painter, apply that second coat of lime himself. They then wait three days for the moisture to evaporate. If they painted before the end of that period, the lime would stain the colors; after that period, the paint would not take well—would not penetrate the mortar, which would be too hard and dry to absorb the paints. Needless to say, the temperature of the air would shorten or lengthen the time needed for the coat to dry to the proper degree before painting.

Before drawing, the master painter smooths the lime finish with a spatula; then, using a string, he determines the dimensions his picture will have. In this picture, in this field of figures, he measures with a compass the dimensions of the various objects he wants to depict. The compass Father Joasaph used was simply a reed bent in two, split down the middle, and fastened with a piece of wood which rejoined the two branches and which closed them or opened them at the painter's will. One of these branches was sharpened to a point; the other was fitted with a brush. A simpler, handier, more economical compass could not be made.

The brush fastened to the end of one leg of the compass is dipped in red; this color is used to trace lines lightly and to sketch the picture. The compass serves principally for drawing halos, heads, and other round parts; everything else is drawn by hand, with the use only of a brush. In a little less than an hour, Father Joasaph had drawn an entire picture before our eyes, and in it were life-size figures of Christ and his apostles; he did this sketch completely out of his head, without any hesitation, without a cartoon or a model, and without even referring to the figures he had already painted in neighboring pictures. I did not see him erase or correct a single stroke, so sure was he of his hand. He began by drawing the principal figure, Christ, who was in the middle of his apostles. First he did the head, then the rest of the body from top to bottom. Next, he drew the first apostle on the right, then the first on the left, then the second on the right and the second on the left, and so on for the others, symmetrically. The painter made his strokes freehand, so to speak, without using a maulstick; this instrument, which painters in our day use, would sink into the wall coating, the lime, which is still moist and too soft. However, when the painter's hand trembles or is tired, he rests it on the wall itself.

Inside these red strokes, which define the outlines of the figures, a subordinate painter spreads a dark background, which he relieves with blue, but in a flat tint like the dark background itself. On this field this painter, a kind of journeyman, draws the draperies and other embellishments. He does not touch the skin areas; these are reserved for the master painter. All the cloth is done and the circular outline of the halo is drawn before the head, hands, and feet.

The master then goes to work on this outline of the figure and does the head. In two stages he spreads a coat of darkish color over the whole face, and fixes the general lines of the face with a still darker color. He paints two heads at a time, moving continuously from one to the other to use up all the color on the brush; moreover, the paint on one head needs time to set in the wall while the other head is being done. Then, with yellow, he does the forehead, cheeks, neck—the flesh properly speaking. A first coat of yellow covers the dark color; a second coat lightens the face. Here nuance is important, and the tint must be right. The painter tries out the intensity of his color on the halo, which has been drawn but not yet filled in, and which serves him as a palette in this case.

After these two layers of yellow, one covering the black and the other lightening the skin, the flesh begins to appear as such. A third coat of this pale yellow, heavier than the first two, produces a general skin tone. The painter does not do the face part by part but all at once; he spreads a coat over the whole face before going on to another coat, the eyes alone excepted, these being reserved for last. Now, with pale green, he softens the dark color he has left in the shadowed portions, already brightened with blue. Then, with yellow, he corrects any encroachments of the green. This green, which tempers the dark color, produces the shadows.

The flesh thus achieved, he makes it live: he applies a rose color to the cheeks, the lips, the eyelids, to heighten their color and breathe life into them. Then, with a dark brown, you see the eyebrows, hair, and beard grow, and there the line of the face stops.

The eyes do not exist yet; they remain dark with the two first general layers of paint. With a darker color, the painter makes the pupil, and the white of the eye with white. Next, a light, delicate rose is used to give the eye its small point of reflected light; sight is kindled and the face sees.

The lips have only been sketched, and the line of the mouth is too dark; the painter lightens and defines the mouth and lips. Then he outlines the whole face with a very dark line to make it stand out. Similarly in the West, in the late Roman period especially, a deep line was scooped out around a sculptured figure to throw it into relief.

A few brush strokes of rose-white are laid on here and there to soften and lighten the brightness of the red in some parts of the flesh. Then, a few strokes of brown to make wrinkles on the older faces. Finally, some strokes of various colors to give the finishing touches to these heads and complete them.

Two heads are painted simultaneously, as I saw Father Joasaph do; it took him hardly an hour for the two. In five days, Joasaph had painted a fresco of the conversion of St. Paul, a picture three meters wide by four high. Twelve human figures and three large horses were deployed on this rather broad expanse. This painting was not a masterpiece, of course, but it was better than what one of our second-rate painters would take six or eight months to do. I even doubt whether our great painters, commissioned to do a religious composition, could do so consistently well; there would be more qualities but also more defects in their work than in the Mount Athos fresco.

When the picture is finished, the artists wait until the lime has dried almost completely; they then finish the figures. They apply gold and silver to the halos and clothing; they enrich the painting with special colors, particularly Venetian blue, and paint the flowers and ornamentation that decorate the interior of the halos, the cloth of the garments, and the background of the picture. For this, the commoner colors used to paint the figures must be quite dry so that they will spoil neither the rarer colors nor the silver and gold.

The figure finished, it is given a name; the person completed, it is baptized and given speech. A special artist, a scribe who works only with lettering, writes the name of the figure inside or around the halo; on the banderole held by the figure he paints the proper holy inscription that the *Guide to Painting* recommends—patriarch, prophet, judge, king, apostle, saint. After that no one touches the work, which is now finished.

These are the careful observations I made in the Esphigmenu church on Mount Athos. While the painter worked, I questioned him, and wrote down on the spot and at his dictation, as it were, what I was seeing and hearing. What I have written just now is the transcription of those notes. It is apparent that the prescriptions of the *Guide* are still observed on Mount Athos, and that the painters do not depart from them noticeably. They almost never use oil, because, as Father Joasaph told me, to paint with oil would require waiting until the wall coating was completely dry, and since the paint would not penetrate the plaster the work would be less durable.

The division of labor, the principle applied in industry with such rewarding results, is practiced in art on Mount Athos. An assistant artist prepares and applies the mortars; two young students mix and dilute the colors. These colors are bought in the village of Karyes, the capital of Mount Athos; they are brought there from Izmir or Vienna, or else they come from France and Italy. A master painter composes the picture, places and linedraws the figures; a student, the first- or second-ranking, does the cloths. The master takes over for the heads, feet, hands—all the flesh. The second-ranking student usually does the embellishments and lays on the gold and silver. A scribe does the lettering. It is because of this division of labor that the sacred artists, using no models and following the *Guide,* can paint such truly remarkable pictures so rapidly. However, only on ordinary pictures and common figures is the work divided. When the subject is the Last Supper or the Crucifixion, when the Pantocrator or the Virgin is to be painted, then the master painter reserves these important figures for himself; he alone puts his hand to them, even for the less important painting. He treats this work with greater care and love. Thus, it is not unusual to see a remarkably well-executed Christ or Virgin in a painting in which the other figures are quite mediocre. The master alone has done the Christ or the Virgin; most of the work on the other parts of the painting has been delegated to students. In France also, in the Middle Ages, the principle of the division of labor was introduced into works of art. When a portal was to be sculptured, the Christ, the divine Persons, and the principal apostles were reserved for the master sculptor; subordinate artists or students were assigned to the other figures. Most of the statues called "Le Beau Dieu" at Chartres, Reims, Amiens, and elsewhere are masterpieces, but alongside them one sees representations of common people or ordinary saints that are rather neutral in quality and sometimes very bad. Yet in earlier times in our art, as today on Mount Athos, the work on a single figure was divided. Hence, in stained-glass windows, those of Chartres among others, depicting sculptors making statues, there are several workers, two for a single figure. One blocks out the body in rough with a hammer, the other models the folds with a chisel; a third is polishing his marble with a long chisel he is pushing with two hands, and a fourth perhaps had sculptured the flesh parts, the head, and the hands.

What we have noted about statues can be said equally of paintings and stained-glass windows. Those great Virgins and our Latin panagia that glow in the central window of the sanctuary facing east are obviously more beautiful than the other figures that file to the right and left of the choir, as can be seen in Notre-Dame de Reims.

A division of labor is an excellent system in industry; it makes for better and quicker production. In art, its results are perhaps not so successful; the work goes more quickly, to be sure, as the painters of Mount Athos demonstrate, but whether it is better is not so certain. Nonetheless, this principle has already been introduced into Western art. In sculpture, the master sculptor makes the model, his assistant works up the figure, and the sculptor finishes it. In a picture that includes landscape, the scenic painter lays out the ground and prepares the drawing, the landscape artist does the nature work, and the historic painter finishes the figures that he had first drawn and a student had then roughed out.

### *Theophilus*

*1.* [Aurichalcum is a natural hydrocarbonate of copper and zinc, the color of verdigris. Under the heading "Zinc," the *Encyclopedia Britannica* (11th ed.) says: "Zinc as a component of brass . . . had currency in metallurgy long before it became known as an individual metal. . . . Pliny explicitly speaks of a mineral . . . as serving for the conversion of copper into aurichalcum. . . ."—Tr.]

*2.* Matthew XXV: 26-27.

### *Cennini*

*1.* The prolix and plundering Romans would doubtless have left nothing behind them without the Greeks, whom they conquered but whom they were incapable of imitating.

*2.* In this connection, I wonder whether rigorous rationalists, given the opportunity, would have the same indulgence for artists as the Pope [Leo X], who was not offended when Raphael painted the story of Psyche on the walls of the Villa Farnesina.

## THE RENAISSANCE

### *Alberti*

*1.* . . . Alberti was probably more of a dilettante than a practising artist. We do know, however, from textual sources (L. B. Alberti, "Della tranquillità dell' animo", *Opera volgare,* Bonucci, ed., I 26) that he made sculpture in wax and clay and perhaps cast these figures in bronze. The anonymous Life refers to his "demonstrations," to portraits in painting and sculpture done in Venice of absent Florentine friends, and to self-portraits.

*2.* This veil, or reticulated net, seems to have been adapted by painters despite current criticism of it implied by Alberti. Leonardo advocates its use as strongly as Alberti. Albrecht Dürer and Holbein the

Younger made minor variations on the net for their use in drawing. In fact, Alberti's invention still appears in popular drawing books. In the fifteenth century the net was probably used in conjunction with squared paper to obtain accuracy in drawing and then later transferred to panel or fresco by means of the same squares.

*3.* As the first to advocate the practice of building the human figure from the bones to the skin, Alberti already prefigures the anatomical researches carried on by Florentine painters in the latter half of the fifteenth century.

*4.* In this passage as in many others Alberti must be read in the context of his historical moment. Although the movements he advocates may seem violent and too varied for our taste, he was almost forced to overstate his position in order to persuade both painter and patron to reject the frozen hieratic figures of Trecento painting. In order to obtain a little vitality and movement he had to ask for much.

Botticelli is perhaps most frequently evoked by this passage, yet the movements of Piero della Francesca's 'Death of Adam'' or of Ghiberti's 'Jacob and Esau' and 'Joseph' panels are closer in spirit to the art of this treasure.

## *Leonardo da Vinci*

*1.* At margin of MS., 'See first the [Ars] Poetica of Horace'.

## *Michelangelo*

*1.* Hollanda misquotes here as elsewhere.

# BIBLIOGRAPHY


ALBERTI, LEON BATTISTA (translated by John R. Spencer), *On Painting*. New Haven: Yale University Press, 1956.

BATAILLE, GEORGES (translated by Austryn Wainhouse), *Lascaux, or the Birth of Art*. Geneva: Skira, 1955.

CENNINI, CENNINO (translated by C. J. Herringham), *The Book of Art of Cennino Cennini*. London: G. Allen, 1899.

DA VINCI, LEONARDO (arranged, rendered into English and introduced by Edward MacCurdy), *The Notebooks of Leonardo da Vinci*. London: Jonathan Cape, 1938.

DE HOLLANDA, FRANCISCO (rendered into English by Aubrey F. G. Bell), *Four Dialogues on Painting*. London: Oxford University Press, 1928.

DIDERON, ADOLPHE NAPOLÉON (translated by Margaret Stokes), *Christian Iconography*. London: George Bell & Sons, 1891.

DOLCE, LODOVICO (translated by Juliette Bertrand), "Dialogue de la Peinture" in *Histoire de la Critique d'Art* (edited by L. Venturi).

DÜRER, ALBRECHT (translated and edited by William Martin Conway, introduction by Alfred Werner), *The Writings of Albrecht Dürer*. London: Peter Owen, 1958.

LOMAZZO, GIAN-PAOLO, *Tracte containing the Artes of curious Painting, Carvinge and Buildinge, and Englished by Richard Haydocke*. Oxford, 1598.

PHILOSTRATUS (English translation by C. Conybeare), *The Life of Appollonius of Tyana*. London: W. Heinemann, 1912. 2 volumes (Loeb Classical Library).

PLINY THE ELDER (translated by H. Rackham), *Natural History*. Cambridge: Harvard University Press, 1938-1962. 10 volumes (Loeb Classical Library).

REINACH, ADOLPHE, *Textes Grecs et Latins rélatifs a l'Histoire de la Peinture ancienne*. (publiés, traduits et commentés). Paris: La Librarie C. Klincksieck et l'Association des Etudes Greques, 1921.

THEOPHILUS (translated from the Latin with introduction and notes by C. R. Dodwell), *The Various Arts*. London, New York: Thomas Nelson, 1961.

VITRUVIUS, POLLIO (edited from the Harleain manuscript 2767 and translated into English by Frank Granger), *On Architecture*. London: W. Heinemann, Ltd. 1931-1934. 2 volumes (Loeb Classical Library).

## *The Editors and Their Book*

# THE EDITORS AND THEIR BOOK

PIERRE SEGHERS was born on January 5, 1906, in Paris, and received his education at the Collège de Carpentras in Vaucluse, France. He is a member of La Société des Gens de Lettres, of La Société des Auteurs et Compositeurs and Le Syndicat des Editeurs and is listed in *Who's Who in France.* Monsieur Seghers is a well-known editor, writer and anthologist, a distinguished critic of the arts.

His published poetic works are: *Bonne-Espérance,* (Ed. de la Tour, 1939) ; *Pour les quatre saisons,* (Poésie 42) ; *Le Chien de pique,* (Ides et Calendes, 1943) ; *Le Domaine public,* (Poésie 45 et Parizeau, Montreal) ; *Le Futur antérieur,* (Editions de Minuit) ; *Jeune Fille,* (1947) ; *Menaces de mort,* (La presse à bras, 1948) ; *Six poèmes pour Véronique,* (Poésie 50) ; *Poèmes choisis,* (Ed. Seghers, 1952) ; *Le Coeur-Volant,* (Les Ecrivains Réunis, 1954) ; *Poèmes choisis,* (Ed. Seghers, 1952) ; *Racines* (Interc. du Livre, 1956) ; *Les Pierres,* (Interc. du Livre, 1958) ; *Chansons et complaintes,* (Ed. Seghers, 1959) ; *Piranèse,* (Ides et Calendes, 1961). His prose works are: *Richaud-du-Comtat,* (Stols, 1944) ; *L'Homme du commun,* (Poésie 44) ; *Considérations, ou Histoires sous la langue.* (Coll. des 150). Included among his widely acclaimed anthologies are: *L'Art Poétique* (in collaboration with J. Charpier) ; *L'Art de la Peinture* (in collaboration with J. Charpier) ; *La France à livre ouvert.*

He has also edited several record albums: *Poèmes,* recited by himself, (Coll. Vox poetica, Monteiro) ; *Douai chante Seghers,* (Ed. B.A.M.) ; *Amours perdues,* (Ed. Véga) ; *Laurent Terzieff dit les poèmes de P. Seghers,* (Ed. Véga).

JACQUES CHARPIER was born on July 5, 1926, in Avignon, was graduated from the Lycée there and later attended l'Institut d'Art et d'Archéologie in Paris. He is at present a literary director for a French publishing house. Like M. Seghers, he is a writer of both poetry and prose. His books of verse are *Paysage du Salut* (Fontaine, 1946) ; *Mythologie du Vent,* (Ed. du Dragon, 1955) ; *Le Fer et Laurier,* (Editions Seghers) ; *Les Deux Aurores* (Editions Seghers). His works of non-fiction are: *Paul Valéry* (Editions Seghers) ; *Charles d'Orleans* (Editions Seghers) ; *St John Perce* (Gallimard) ; and *L'Art Poétique* (Editions Seghers), which he edited in collaboration with M. Seghers. He is now at work on an essay in poetry.

THE ART OF PAINTING FROM PREHISTORY THROUGH THE RENAISSANCE (HAWTHORN, 1964) was designed by Betty Binns and completely manufactured by The Vail-Ballou Press, Binghamton, New York.

*(Continued on next page)*

The body type is De Vinne, a type named after T. L. De Vinne and cut in 1894 by Gustav Schroeder. The display face is Torino, a modern English design (1908) from an Italian foundry. The color inserts were printed by the Istituto Italiano d'Arti Grafiche, Bergamo, Italy.

A HAWTHORN BOOK